Companion

Christine Berger

Letters

Concrescent Letters

For information contact:
Concrescent Letters, an imprint of Concrescent LLC
Richmond CA, USA
info@Concrescent.net

ISBN: 978-0-9903927-5-0

Library of Congress Control Number: 2018942561

There are words in the English language that are very rich in meaning, one of them is the word Companion, which I have titled this book.

To me it covers the range from the Holy Guardian Angel, the Higher Self, teachers, guides, friends, even Deities that help me walk my talk in this lifetime.

In addition, I love Josh Whedon's Companion, who was lover, counselor, and wise woman combined with true elegance and grace.

All of these meanings have play in this book, which I am dedicating to Aphrodite, that aspect of the God who has not to date given me a name, but is represented as He speaks in the book, and the Companions of the world who give their lives to Love.

In my personal life, it has been the healing in intimate relationships which has been the hardest to come by and had the greatest impact upon me.
I am deeply grateful to all those who have loved and been loved by me. You make my life sweet when everything else feels like it is falling apart.

This book is dedicated to Aphrodite and the God who has appeared in many forms, as well as all Companions, wherever they may be in the Verse.

At the Beginning

The Player, The Priestess, and The Lover

Part I 01-26-15

When she went to the Lover
She was still wearing the battle-scars from the Player
Though she never thought of him unless it was to look at
Whatever was left to heal
In contrast to the Lover he now crossed her mind
But not as the person who personified Him as much as
The Player by definition

From a vantage point of compassion
Which is the bonus package that comes when
She answers Love's demands by keeping her heart open
She understands now that the Player
Is a damaged Lover, one who when hurt at some point
Decided to close the door, and let only enough Love in
To be able to Play the game
Which is all about control
Now that she is not bleeding from Him
She understands the tragedy of the Player
As she knows you either play to win in Loving
or you lose with the loss of the ability to either give or
receive it

She cried in the night because she was ashamed that
she had let
the Player seduce her into loving him and a kind of bondage
Yet she remembers the rare glimpses of the broken lover
inside Him
and knows that the bonds were as much for him and his
being overshadowed
By the one who controlled him as anything else

She remembers after the Player left that he told her he
knew she would be stronger
When he was gone
and realizes that was maybe the only time she knew he
was telling the truth

But when she was ashamed and realized that part of her
wanted to run From the Lover because He made her feel
again and her heart open
and her body embrace desire
That she would not under any circumstances do so
Because He bore the gift of healing that she had been
asking for
and she felt into who she would be were she whole
once again
Stronger from loving the Player, and the intensity with
which she gave of all of her being
her heart, her mind, her spirit and her body
and she knows that there is no one nor anything that can
take that
Which she is within
That which allows her to look at herself and say
Priestess
Even though sometimes she wishes she had never met him.

The Player, The Priestess, and The Lover

Part 2 01-28-15

The Priestess sits in the stillness of the clearing
Her spine straight, seat firm on the forest floor
She reflects on the path that has unfolded
Bringing her here
and seeks vision of that which lies before her

Her journey has been long
sometimes simple and fast
sometimes burdened with lessons none too easy
Yet always the twin currents of Love and Passion
The tender mercies of the Gods and Goddesses
she serves were present
Always visible, though sometimes more murky in her sight
Than others

She tells her story:

When I was young I was ignorant
of the ways of men and the ways of the Gods
I had heart and fire
But not much sense
Were it not for the Gods I would have been lost
But they unfurled my fate as I stumbled along
A child who had not learned to love herself
and so was inadequate in loving others
Yet still there was always one guiding light in my life
One friend in form, one teacher
Since I was not yet aware of the strength from within

There were periods of wild adventure
and service to Love itself in ways many would find abhorrent
But if I knew nothing else, I knew how to follow
The glimmers of guidance of my Mistress
Who said go here, serve in this way
Not forever, but for now
Many the crossroads, the times when I was stripped of my
Outer support system, and felt completely abandoned
When there was nothing I could do but to let go completely
Relying on my Heart and the rising knowledge that the Universe
did have my back

I married and to this day I do not know
if the purpose of that was to bring a child
A daughter into the world
Since the doctors had told me it was impossible
and the child grew to be a fine woman in her own right
Though our bond now is not what my heart has longed for
I am proud of her

Lovers were few and far between
Though the path of sacred sex revealed itself bit by bit
and Passion and Love woke the Muse within me
(and these gifts were priceless)
My heart broke over and over
Yet each time revealed itself stronger and deeper and with
more capacity
To love
When the Player left me in the dust and a period of
initiation left me in the wastelands
of Satori
I sought to rebuild myself
As Priestess whole and grateful and ready to give myself
In whatever way called to do so.

I have new practices in the last few years
A plethora of Gods and Goddesses
That I worship daily in offerings of joy
Reiki and poetry keep me sane
Support comes when I am brought low
and I have a tribe of like minded ones who I adore
Slowly I have realized that my mistake in my youth was
Chasing love in order to receive it
When it was always inside waiting to be released
and the key to that was to let it flow as a gift
It would come and it would go and it would tell me of
its journeys

Then all paths of Love and Sex and Service aligned
and I met the Lover
Not for satisfaction's sake
But for Healing and instruction
in how to meld the Lover and Priestess within
How to prepare to make that the focus of my life
and to share it with all I am led to for that reason.

The Player, The Priestess, and The Lover

Part 3 01-28-15

I hear you and your stories
of your life and what you think it means
Yet I tell you now, though you may seek a Lover
Kind and gentle
That until you are ready to surrender everything to Love
In all its aspects
What you look for will elude you

Love is like Nature Herself
Fierce, relentless and savage
Especially when married to Passion
You who seek the Union with these
Must be certain your house is clean
Your mind calm
Your emotions detached
Your body whole
and I warn you once again
Be careful what you ask for

You think that you seek only to Serve
But I see into your hidden heart and I say
Make certain that you have no agenda
Before you take another step on this path
Because I rule it in all my faces
As does the Goddess
and you have no idea what you are getting yourself into

However;
If you are willing to sacrifice everything
To let go of all your illusions of self and admit how
little you know
About Self
If you are willing to have your boundaries torn down
over and over again
If and when you are ready to bleed for Love
and wait until she deems you ready

Then come to Me without fear.

Winter
Yule
2014

Desire Comes

02-09-15

Desire comes unbidden
It has no sense of timing and can strike anywhere
It sometimes has discrimination but often not
It can render a grown woman with freedom on her mind
Susceptible to some girlish teenage persona which she
thought she left long behind
It can tease it can thwart it does not respect careful thought
It has no impulse control in fact not only does it blow
up impulse control
But it has a good time doing so

It can arise in a crowded room
Stirred by the one most inappropriate, unlikely and
unsuitable person
Available - or even worse, sometimes unavailable and
uninterested
It can crawl into the spaces in your dreams
your practice
Disturb your meditations
mess with your body chemistry
It will have its way with you - it will exist when and
where it pleases

Yet the reins are fully in your hand, Priestess
You can walk toward or away from any object of Desire
Well knowing that the fire Desire ignites is your birthright
And dependent on no man nor woman to keep it burning
Satisfaction can come in a myriad of flavors
On the physical plane and/or on others
This danger that has you trembling helplessly
Is only your recognition that though free will is always
yours to own
Desire can still make you quiver and shake and yearn and burn
Whenever it damn well feels like it.

Might as well let down your resistance and enjoy the ride.

Playing with TNT

02-11-15

The music beat through my body
My partner and I well matched
The energies which had been building for days
Peaking to the point
Where it was no longer comfortable
and I not finding the space to let go and surrender to them
was like a child woman with Desire and Sexuality the Master
This transformative force is more than often given credit for
This vulnerability a mix of an ancient innocence
and the residue of all the times in any lifetime
Where I misused beauty and sex and neglected the pure
essence
of just loving

You were gracious
Exhausted yet sleepless I wanted you to come back
But it would not have been a good time
I took to my bed and sought the release I needed
Like a tidal wave it came and I thought surely I would drown
Only to be tossed upon the shore
I could have drifted off to sleep
But the candle on Loki's altar kept going out
and the neighbor boy was howling at the Universe
So sleep eluded me

As I lay there I contemplated
the responsibility that comes with being a Firecaster
I will not allow my desire for pleasure to interfere
With fledgling friendships nor any relationships with tribe
or within tribe
As kith and kin are second in importance only to the Gods
and past history has left deep scars from my losses therein

So I leave it to you, dear Sir
to work with me in understanding which boundaries need
to be leveled
and which ones treasured and respected
We are none of us alone on this journey
and I would seek the Grace and Blessing of the Gods
upon the journey of Sacred and Profane Sex united
and risk not a single second of a pained heart
With anyone as we all take the only gamble that really matters
Betting our all for Love

Fire in the Head

02-17-15

Someone in a gathering used this expression
To refer to the experience of completely being within
the presence of a particular Goddess
But I find it expresses perfectly the transition this morning
From a low energy, almost depressed state
Where I sat rejecting thoughts that I do not will to be
in my being nor my environment
To the wham that hit my head reading a blog
From a priestess I deeply respect on sacred sexuality
and a video by Ani DiFranco accompanying it
and then boom
The top of my head came off

I wait now for the inspiration and Presence to meld and write

I will not allow you to demean yourself
To deny Love or to split it up into pieces of giving and receiving
Because in truth it is your home, it is where you live
and breathe
It is your life and your joy and all that you are
If humans could finally stop this thinking of Love as
something outside of themselves
Something that comes and goes rather than this Fiery
life-giving force at the center
Above and below and irresistibly all that is
Perhaps their desire to change their world could
manifest so fast that it would knock
them
Off their feet and upon their asses while they laughed
and cried in infinite relief
Saying "we are home, and now we see we never left"

I ask you to take your moments of peak experience
While the taste of love and gratitude is fresh upon your tongue
Draw those experiences and how they feel deep into every cell of your body
Embrace and integrate them with spirit and heart and mind
Let them serve as a fountain of joy and comfort
Do what is necessary to maintain the fitness of the temple that is your body
and do not allow the curve balls that the world throws at you
Or your own shadow work
To cause you to deny their reality nor to disrupt your core certainty
Yet keep their glow close at hand

It takes only a small spark of the Holy Fire within
To start a bonfire where all can gather
Again and again

Think yourselves not alone
The bonds between Gods and men are strengthening each and every day

I Triggered Myself

02-19-15

Ouch
I had to take the walk outside even though
We are having a long lunch free from work for the
Chinese New Year
And I had not intended to do so

I had been myself
With someone I like
A companion
Who I know but do not know for long
Nor necessarily well outside of a given framework
I spoke the desire for continuity in friendship (and
maybe more)
Gave myself about half an hour and then freaked

The walks are dedicated to the Gods Brigid and Pan
So I asked for their help in sorting out my angst
First, if I am myself, and not cruel or thoughtless in
some way
But merely opening
Then if someone, friend or lover, runs
That is for the best

Now, the triggers
Insecurity
Due to my track record in love affairs
I do not trust myself, nor my instinct to be accurate
However; at the same time, I do trust both the Gods
And the two men who have moved my heart and spirit and body
Currently

Deprivation
I have done without lovers for long stretches in my life
I am tired of that aspect in my life being empty
Both my own needs and my heart and my desire to be whole
In all areas of my life as Priestess
And perhaps to carry that path of loving as a large part
of my spiritual path
Next year
I do not want that empty spot in my life

So I can choose to honor and trust the timing of the Gods
And live each day the best I can, giving what I can but
accepting
That this part of me that has been hurt
Who has not given love well nor often
Who is both lonely and loving
Giving and selfish
Is part of being human
I need to cut her some slack so that we can
communicate
With each other and continue to grow

Guilt
I found guilt sitting there entwined with Passion and
Pleasure
He could give me no reason for his presence
I explained that I have not infringed on another woman's man
All is above board and all parties aware of me
And probably at least on the part of the men aware of
What I want - what price I will pay but also what
price I am not willing to have
Anyone else pay
I am as clean as I am capable of being
Guilt does not belong here and now

Finally
I spoke to the God and Goddess again
I could not promise that I would never be afraid again
But I did commit to YES
Yes to loving even though it hurts sometimes
Yes to giving without worry for the result
Both of heart and flesh
Mind and spirit
Yes to receiving what is offered from loving and
beautiful men
Who are Priests and worthy of both love and respect
Yes to that part where the God may say
Stand on this precipice and then leap with abandon

I know that this path is mine to tread
Though my will is always free to choose
There are also doors that are open now
Because of choices I have made over the past
Four decades
To not walk through them is to deny who and what I am
To deny the best of me
And to deny the God and Goddess who have heard the
prayers of heart and spirit
And brought me here

So I say YES

Rebirthing the Priestess

02-20-15

It takes the right set and setting
As we used to say in the sixties
Before dropping acid
The environment clean and natural
A living altar
The right companions
Of like mind with sacred intent and holy hearts
These journeys within our deepest beings are best planned
With care if the outcome is to be what we desire

My body is humming like a honeybee since last night
Yet the touch between us was mind and heart and spirit
As the body yielded itself to absolute desire
And the heart opened as a flower in full bloom
Nurtured by loving friends and then our brief time alone
These flames of desire
Blended with the calm depths of water
Kept us both awake
Until you soothed me with a story

Set and setting between lovers is woven
Of trust, connection and understanding
As a companion told me recently
It is not desire or freedom to love that I was lacking
It was the right person
It takes a strong man or woman
To create that atmosphere where their partner can take
the leap
Into free fall
Allowing love to Burn
The sacred flesh to release itself to the abandon
Of desire
Without fear or the lust for results

When the little teenage girl within raises her head
And asks
"Is it safe?"
I calm her and tell her the only thing that would not be safe
Would be to stand against this tidal wave
This bonfire
Would be to offer resistance
To what the Priestess has craved for a lifetime

Don't Give a Damn 'Bout My Reputation

02-24-15

This first line of the song keeps playing in my head
Which usually means it is a key to unlocking something
So with help from above and below I will try and break
it down

It also ties to a recovery saying
" What other people think about you is none of your business"
That too has always made my brain stop in its tracks
And is another part of the key.

So I have to question
How do I value myself
If the things that I call identifying marks about me
Were taken away or unrecognized or unvalued by others
Where would that leave me
Another keyword is sovereignty
Also still very mysterious to me

So let me experiment with myself on this
I think of myself as mystic, polytheist, witch
Healer and poet
I am cisgender female
Apparently I am polyamorous
Although it has taken years for that to be a
comfortable I.D.
And I am still slowly trying to fully integrate that.
Which of these things would fall away if no one
recognized them as connected to me

The first three, mystic, polytheist and witch
Are at the core of my m.o. in life
They determine my private practice
My way of thinking and being with the Universe
And the ethical framework which keeps me happy with myself
So if no one acknowledged them or understood them
I would be painfully alone (and have been there)
But I probably would not fall apart
Maybe go live in a cave somewhere
If there were no social network to support me
But without practice and the Gods I would not want to
be here
And would no doubt find a way to exit.

Healer and poet
Both gifts priceless to me in this lifetime
Because they give me purpose and a reason for being
On those dark of the soul type passages where I wonder
Why I am here and if it is at all worth it or of benefit
If no one acknowledged them or understood them
My healer's heart would break but I would still use Reiki
It would find a way to get out into the world
If no one ever read a poem of mine
Or told me that it made them happy or sad or reacted in
some way
I would still be compelled to write
But if I were a hermit, the rich fertile ground of living
life with others
Would eliminate a powerful impetus to create and bring forth
If the Muse abandoned me I would probably dry up and
get old
Without Reiki I would also probably do the same.

This is a good exercise
Because the day will come when I am stripped bare
Of the clothing of body and personality and such identifiers
What does the Universe tell me will be left if anything
Love
And only Love.

So this idea of sovereignty seems to me to be
Among other things
The ability to stand alone if necessary
Without an outer support system
And say
" I am here"
" I am alive and by that fact alone I have value"
" I love and respect myself regardless of what others
think"
" I hold myself to the highest standards, my free will is
my birthright, my ever-loving heart my admission ticket"

If you know me and love me that gladdens my heart
If you do not know me and hate and dismiss me, none of
my business beyond holding my boundaries
If you know me and love me not, though you may break
my heart, again, that is neither my business nor my issue.

It Is Ok to Fail

02-26-15

It is ok to fail
It is ok to fall on your ass
It is ok to make mistakes in how you speak or act
With other people
You can make amends
You can resolve to listen better
Welcome to this glorious mess
Of being Spirit in form
As a human being
At work I found myself foggy
Confused
And awkward
So I sat with it
Yep
Sometimes I am all of those things
Went inside and asked for help
The clarity came
I let go of any embarrassment about these human
qualities
That do not thrill others when they are busy and
stressed
As one of my favorite people now gone used to say
"It's OK"

I am learning, finally after many many years of beating myself up
With that perfectionist voice whispering in my ear from my youth
To be gentle
And in being gentle with myself
May I also remember to be gentle with others
Many times we cause hurt unwittingly
I have been horror struck more than once
At being called to account for my actions or speech
And caught totally unaware of how I affected others
Losing all of my outer support system over a decade ago
Made me cautious and more inclined to take care
With friends and loved ones
As if friendships were made of the finest porcelain china
More fragile than we sometimes know
I never want to break relationships again mindlessly
As the heart pays a terrible price for that on all sides.

Living in the Moment

02-27-15

Neptunian influences both call and seduce me
Gift me with a fluidity
Make me recognize certain gifts that might be hidden at
another time
But also challenge me to be present
The diffused energy of Neptune calling me to swim with
the dolphins
Of my internal seascape
Does not help me when at work or driving home and
needing to deviate
From the habitual route

Good in meditation
But not so much in offerings
Where direct individual focus is necessary

So my counterbalance is to sharpen focus on the moment

Two places where this works very well
Physical relations and dancing
Involving the body allows for both fluidity and attention
I love a particular blues venue available online
Because the DJ is both gifted and very hard at work to connect
Tune to tune
He builds the energy and I dance building the endorphins
Until the dance is moving me and there is an ecstasy of
the body

The dance of sexuality is that combination of responsive attention
And the flow directed by body and magic
Each time to me has always been a journey
An adventure
A discovery
Until those times when all that I am succumbs to the primal force of it
And like a child on the roller coaster it is all about the ride.
And for my ever loving Priestess heart
It is all about the loving....

When Boundaries Shift, Where is the Middle?

03-02-15

As an ecstatic by nature
When currents are strong and carry me willingly
To push limits previously set
At what point do I say uncle, enough?
These rapid changes embracing us all are like the rapids
Hurling over rocks in a waterfall
So easy to let go and let that crazy wild flow carry us.

Yet at a certain point the body is tired
The mind overwhelmed
Even Spirit within this form needs Silence and
Detachment
Just one step back
To check in with the heart
To be certain that there has been no careless moment
With another's will, or boundaries
No careless speech
No selfish agenda
Without standing as if in another's shoes

Repercussions that result from inattention
Are not excusable
If I am to stand as Priestess
I cannot allow myself to be unaware (to the best of my ability)
Of how my being in the world affects others
There are actions spontaneous that are Spirit led
Those do not worry me
But within the throes of passion
Be it within the body or the mind or heart
There must be some part that can watch and say
Hold back here
Let go here
Check yourself
Hear the words before you let them loose from your mouth
Do not let the torrential waters sweep you away
without that anchor
Which the Earth below you is always offering.

(She says " sometimes you worry too much,
sometimes you hold too tight,
I have given you the key – do not lust for results.
Mind the counsel of the heart and listen for my voice.")

I Got It Bad

03-02-15

When did it happen?
When did my body tied to mind and heart
Accept your touch and your Being
As a long lost friend,
As something long hungered for
As a need that makes me shiver
and want to run
Unable to deny that loving gives us power over each other
It holds and comforts us
shakes up the stale and frees the hidden
Bares parts of us that maybe we are not sure should be seen
Yet I cannot do anything but surrender to it
I can feel loving you is as natural as breathing

When did that happen?

This need for you terrifies me
I have felt like this before and thought it would nearly
kill me
Yet the truth is that I survived
I even thrived after the wounds healed and scabs fell off
Then there were barren days
As I wondered was it ever possible again?
Was I doomed to love friends and not know a lover's
touch again
In even the deepest terror that terror of being known and
seen and naked
I would not give up a moment of pleasure or pain
as this heart drinks from you and your gifts of feeling
once again

Only a fool would refuse the gamble of loving
in fear of what is fleeting or what is deep
after all life is fleeting and all is deep

When You Say Yes to Me

03-03-15

When you say yes to me
I melt inside
It makes me want to give you everything
To bring joy and happiness to you
With your generous heart and Spirit
I am trying to convey in words how this feels
I want to remember so that my Yeses flow easy and free
As that joy rides on both giving and receiving
You surprise and delight me
I don't know when I learned to expect No
I think that I have been trained that way
And maybe as my heart becomes more willing and capable
of its own Yeses
Or maybe because it already has
The Universe is dropping them into my lap
Like golden drops of sunlight made solid
Or maybe it is just you

Changes, Destination Unknown

03-03-15

You ask me do I know what is coming
How it will lift me change me leave me gasping
How it will challenge me
Make me tremble make me sweat
Take me to my limits
Cause my heart to burst open wider than before
Until I know that it has no boundaries
Cause my body to strengthen and become healthier
As it too rises to the occasion as you give instruction
For proper tending of its needs

I answer, No
All I know to do is to let go
To listen as well as I know how
To keep silent until the words force themselves forth
Driven by heart and Spirit
Meditation has become my sanctuary
First approached early in the morning
Before anything can distract me
Though staying only a few moments before You kick me out
In those moments all is perfect
Especially the one just before that quick exit
The one of silence and embrace and melding

These days, I know less
And feel more
I burn from a fire that has risen from spark to flame
I hunger for the deepest waters
The deepest connections
The heart of the forest
The rhythm of the sea
The torrential downpour of rain
And the embrace of sun as it penetrates my skin

I hunger for the rituals that feed us
That slough away all the crap the world tries to bind us with
Until we remember and see once again
That there is no membrane separating us from each other
Nor no world that we have not and are not shaping now

The ecstasies you let me taste are more than I can bear
Indeed more than I can bear without being changed
permanently transformed into
The best of whatever this is that I am
And that is exactly what I desire the most
And what drives me to share all that I am here and now
Within the succor of Perfect Gratitude

Emotional Rescue

03-12-15

As if wandering a path in the deepest forest
With overgrowth and brambles obscuring the way
There has been an overpowering clearing and experiencing of
Emotions that have surfaced in the last week
They rise like the foam of the sea
Rides the surface of its wave
Demanding acknowledgment
The heart demanding healing

The impact was great enough to knock me off my feet
To manifest a congestion in the heart and infection in
the head
As if to illustrate in living color
How well body and mind – spirit and heart are aligned
You may attempt to think of them as single and isolated portions
Of what you think of as self
But they are one only.

What I think of a situation arises from how I feel
The harm done to a sister impacts me
If there is a common denominator
It influences my experiences even though not immediately mine
This holds true for all of us though it is easier to see
in a close relationship

I float in a kind of limbo
A detached observer of the last few months
Of the highs and the lows
Owning none of them I witness their effects
And I do own my responsibility in thought, word and action
As everything ripples out from where I stand
Just as I receive the incoming tides constantly

This morning, as is often my way
I invited a Deity to aid me in meditation
The chest still tight and more closed than was comfortable
The center seat for Love also not as open as usual
At the last minute I remembered the admonition to formally invite in
The help I sought
From Brigid came the image of a hand burning red and hot with sacred fire
Which She placed over my heart

At her touch there was a jolt of release
On all levels
And I could breathe again

These next two weeks are intense for all who live here
I am mindful that although I know results are up to the Holy Powers
In tandem with past choices and present desire
How I step each step these days will have more impact than usual
So I will do my best to tether the impulse to give vent to anger or irritation
As outer fire poking my fire is prone to cause

I am letting go of what I thought I knew yesterday
And letting the heaven's upheaval shake it out as it will
The die for much of this cast long ago
Like my younger self I am remembering with the tidal waves that there are no escape from
Surfing is the best m.o.

She Holds Me With a Light Tether

03-16-15

It is as I have requested
That towing line to keep me from going too far off course
Most of the time, at worst, the slightest tug will realign me
With my purpose
Her purpose
The work at hand
When I am willing (in truth I am nearly always)
And able (this gets a little trickier)
To let the Heart and Love fully lead
Things flow
Even when being used for healing in painful territory

Sometimes I get stuck though
Shadow work not faced in the early stages
Can become a three headed monster in my mind
Although that is not where it lives
In those times She will take the sharpest scalpel
Look me dead in the eyes and say
Are you ready?
Be ready to let go upon my signal

Sometimes the time it takes to process
Leaves me squirming like a butterfly on a pin
But at the ultimate surrender and release
I am pleasantly surprised when I find no traces
Of something which had bothered me for years

Yesterday, as a result of energies of love making
Building and being held deliberately, an epiphany was
triggered without effort on my part
I was with a dear friend
Helping him pack some things into the car
Barefoot because I hate wearing shoes if I do not have to

I stepped onto the sidewall, then the grass
And Her presence filled the entire space surrounding me
Gazing at the sky I felt the immensity of it
Gazing at my feet happily rooted in the earth
I felt the depth of it
Held so completely and tenderly by Her
As my recognition of the experience was made fully conscious
I delighted in my own space, small yet mine
My place within Her a joyous homecoming
And the moment Divine.

Out of the Blue

03-17-15

It calls to me
In the midst of a busy work day
It calls to me when I am driving
Or taking care of mundane tasks
It calls to me when I am drifting off to sleep
Or slowly registering the morning alarm

It approaches as a warm energy steeping into my heart
From all directions and none it simply is rising
I feel it now touching my root chakra
Making certain that the fires though banked are active
And healthy
It lays a blanket of calmness from Spirit over my mind
And teases the emotions into a lightness
As these little stresses of the world
Are not mine to own
Nor the weight of heavy burdens mine to carry
Compassion arises, and takes notes
To send to source in prayer and meditation
As it reminds me to take care of this precious child here
(me!)
While watching the wheel turn
(oh so very fast these days)

It speaks to me thus:

" Everything is changing
And the energies of revolution and transformation
That you embraced ecstatically when very young
You need to receive just as easily and naturally now
Remembering that the life force itself is intense
breathtaking change
That the vitality of it is aligned thus
Know that your essence is one and the same
Your body perfectly capable of riding these changes

Once again I say
All you have to do is let go, throw your hands up like a
giggling child
And watch as this marvelous show unfolds"

The Hunger

03-18-15

A lot of reading today
About how others feel about the Holy Powers in their lives
About relationships
How they begin
What is desired
And how humans approach the Gods

When I think of these things
There rises in me a deep hunger
A desire for closeness, for relationship
I do not know that I even WANT to define
The relationship
Besides one of Priestess
I want to get close to Hermes for example
I want to give love, respect, service and put any abilities I have
Known or unknown into the offerings I make Him
Because standing before those altars with a match and
an invocation
The offering is always me to Them

What do I want to get back?
Knowledge of Them
Of what They want in the world and our part down here
To bring that about
What co-creation is and how to strengthen its
effectiveness here
How to expand myself to love more and better
And how to both surrender and hold my strand of the
web in autonomy
Which I know is not a contradiction but sure as heck
is a work in progress

My horoscope today said the emphasis was on my
relationship with a lover
To speak about what we each wanted to see; where that melded
And where it needed work
Is it weird that I find it easier to talk about relating to
the Holy Powers
Than this lover and I,
With its rich flavor of something brand new and
something I should already know my way around?
In the realm of man and woman stuff
I almost always feel inadequate and uninformed

I am going to take a leap with this one as well
Diving into it and doing my best to navigate each day
Truly, I do not know any other way to be here.

In the Clearing

03-19-15

There is a place between the worlds
Sometimes in a dream, night or day it exists as well as
In meditation
It may be a meadow or a clearing in deep forest
There may be a huge oak in it
or flowers scattering the meadow
there may be a brook or stream
sunlight or moonlight
stars on a clear night
It may be balmy and warm
but usually not chilly
The appearance of it matters less
than the feel of it
the spaciousness and perfect groundedness of it
The taste of eternity there
This the safe place for the truth of self, Self and Gods
Higher Self and HGA
this the sacred meeting place for all

If poetry came from somewhere it would drift down
from there
if the ease of body, spirit and heart arose
in sacred dance or lovemaking
where the body is a fluid being of passionate energy
The clearing would be the foundation for the release of it
Just as a child will take its first steps with courage
Knowing that the shelter of a mother's arms is close at hand

I thought today of passion
of the fire that consumes but does not destroy
of the body becoming liquid and fluid and totally receptive
To the Lover
This year has blessed me
with a renaissance of feeling and loving
A joy at vulnerability - mine and others
A gentleness and compassion
overruling my needs and letting the Heart lead the way
A sloughing off of damages both real and imagined
and yes
Even an acceptance that the hardest lessons
in Love made me more human and more capable
to be the lover I want to be
more able to be with an equal partner

There is a new commitment to Love rising each and everyday
I await the timing, but each day brings hints and pokes
The Goddess presented Herself recently as the Universe
in a brief vision
The God who asked me two months ago
Was I willing to come to Him without fear and risk it all
Is coming out of the shadows
With a terrible and tender smile upon his face
And eyes deep and ancient with Love
My No has been drowned within tears of gratitude
and only Yes echoes through my mind

The clearing has become a circle
With a Maypole at the center
Dancers in their vibrant colors
Weave the wyrd for us all
While I stand on the edge spellbound.

Soon, they whisper, soon
the work will begin

Spring 2015

Sailor and the Sea

03-21-15

The water calls
when the fire has burned and I am nearly crispy
tired and a little frazzled from its relentless heat
Needing the soothing of the deep places
As these dual currents so primary to my nature
Need blending once again

It is those deep places those currents
The waters calm beneath the surface
That call me

Just as hidden depths in a man
Draw me out and towards him
It is mystery and revelation
That both taunt and satisfy
the quiet places within me

Music has seduced me and drawn out my Spirit
for over fifty years now
Ours the generation that was birthed and rebirthed
through it
Our anthems our odes to awakening consciousness
Our battle cry and our comfort when all else failed
It carried an inner revolution for us and we served It
as best we could

Music is life blood
If water nourishes the land and calms the fire
Music heals reveals stimulates and opens
all that we are
it brings us together
in a way that few things can

These days I feel destiny kissing me lightly on the brow
and certainly She is welcome
There is an inner surge that arises within me
an ageless joy and expectation
Knowledge that I am being changed
and only for the better
and a new willingness
To let these forces flow within and around me
Something new is giving birth to Itself
and it is doing it through us

Thank you for letting me see you.

To My Erstwhile Potential Lover

03-24-15

I don't want your money
Nor a ring upon my finger
I don't care if we live together

Though you would be a lovely neighbor

I don't care to take up all your time and energy
I value my freedom as much as you do yours
I don't want to own you or to control you
Though on occasion if you let me persuade you
You may make me purr

What I do want
Is to feel the connection between us that is like a live wire
Burning in a way that opens worlds within who we are together
I want to know some of the secrets of your heart
As I am built to share my own
I want to know what in this world, this life,
Thrills you
Makes you rise up from your bed with a smile on your face
What you give to the whole of life because you must,
because who you are demands it
And once in awhile
I want you to tell me how I fit into your Universe

I guarantee that I will tell you how and why you fit
into mine.

Any contract we engage in will be a contract for heart
and spirit
I will not have the law of the land determine the
boundaries of mine again
I am ready to engage in the adventure of us
But please just know I am not a halfway gal
My speeds are adjustable
But clearly there is an off and an on switch
Be sure what you want before you turn me on.

Off Balance—
Who Wins, Love or Fear?

03-24-15

Today I woke up an hour and a half late
having somehow managed to not set the alarm
I am all in disarray though I made it to work on time
My morning practice disrupted
Meditation distracted by turbulence in a sea of emotions
and a questioning of why I do what I do sometimes
an 8 year clean and sober anniversary is a fine time to do this

A new aspect of self has been coming through this year
A youthful presentation of Priestess to Aphrodite
Who is like me when I was younger
But more fearless, more aggressive and sometimes a bit
terrifying
In her openness
Yet her heart is generous
Her Spirit daunting in its free expression
She who is me but feels sometimes not like me
Is in all likelihood the best I have to offer here
Although how she instinctively maps and navigates the
terrains of life
Does at times leave alternate and outdated modes of
personality
who are not quite ready to loosen their control
a bit shaken and a tiny bit terrified

How can one possibly evaluate one's own growth?
Remember as a kid when they told you that you were
going through a growth spurt
I remember those times as awkward as if you were
growing into a new skin
before the old one had been shed
Perhaps that is a good analogy
As I feel a warmth and calmness rising from within

I have no idea if this way of being fearless
and heart-centered with total abandon
is all that it is cracked up to be
Sometimes I wonder if I am delusional
or I get lost in the power of emotions that arise from
nowhere
and tend to capsize me
Yet the rougher the waters the more inclined I am to let go
I can sense something greater than I handling the rudder
All I can do is stay awake
and note the course corrections.

Oh Hell Yeah

03-27-15

I like your voice and the way you know
How to let your music flow and take a room full
On a ride, energies running wild and hot
Reminding of the joy and the rush of it
These skills prevalent in my youth
The taste of it reminds me of what has been missing

I love the way you move, by design crossing the realities
I love that you make time for me
I love that you always respond with heart and kindness
You make me happy
Where no one else that I know could pull it off
You open my eyes to possibilities
neither seen nor imagined
making space in the sweet depth of the night
After hours of working your ass off

I love the man I feel under that sweet tasty image
From the beginning I knew there was no BS
Hiding under the well done persona
Easy to see who you are has
worth and depth and breadth to it,
Infused with Spirit

I love that you leave joy and peace
Heat and heart behind for me
It is no wonder I keep coming back for more

Now at work with the blues
Making me wanna holler and sneak in a hip move here
and a hip move there
within the cubicle jungle

You make me want to give you everything I am
You are precious.

No Easy Way Out

03-30-15

She smiles at me with a sidelong glance
and then chuckles softly:

«I hear that you are dismayed that there is no loophole
No easy way out when the work I give you becomes
difficult
Were you not warned that serving Us would demand
everything that you are
Would challenge you, strip you down to your bare bones
turn you inside out and blast your boundaries open
Can it be that you still thought to seek only the bliss
and pleasure of My world
without paying dues at the same time?

You who swear your fealty before my altar each day
and in other worlds as well
cannot be so simple minded
I know that you know I listen
Have I not held you when you were shaking and broken down?
Have I not instructed you in the ways to get healing
and led you there by the hand?
I wonder, you who have sought Me for so long,
Are you really turning coward even before things get
interesting

I am teaching you
I have brought forth a younger and stronger aspect of you
It is my energy that sustains her and guides her
So that you can receive all the information and tools
that you need
I can feel you now as your spine straightens
and your heart trembles at My presence
and Joy obliterates your fears
Truly, would you turn from me now because there is no
easy answer?

Foolish little one
There is one answer
The one that you have always known
The one that grabs you tightly now and holds you fiercely
Surrender all to Me
Surrender all to Love
Surrender and take the leap and watch what happens
Leave behind the mortal cares and fears
There is no room for them if you are to serve Me and
the Lord≫

≪You are welcome.≫

Shards of Ice

04-04-15

As if pierced and frozen the heart hurts
To the point that I take the child's pose on the floor
Hoping for some relief some spark of the holy fire within
That which we call Love
That which we know is what sustains Life
The Source
That place of contact the line goes out from there and
The energy that comes up from earth and down from
the heavens
Alights and dwells there

If I am not in the state of Loving
Then I am frozen immobile stuck and all systems haywire
I can search for reasons why I am out of sync
But like a deer dying from a mortal wound
reasons will not heal
to the traveler hopelessly lost in the desert
thirsty for water
the path to the oasis is what matters
Not the one which had obscured its presence

I am broken bits
and I am whole
I am disruption and chaos
and I am that which is reconciled and at peace
I am hard to love even for myself
and I am easy to love like the child of my own flesh
I am all contradictions
and I am the perfect resolution of them as one taste
I am that which is frozen and static
and I am that which flows like raging water
and burns like a towering bonfire

I am pain to myself as my heart contracts
and I am a release such as the first breath of life
When the heart is open and expands

Wherever I am in this moment
I seek to be found and accepted in my totality
as myself to me
as that which even I cannot understand wholly
so that maybe, just maybe
I can love and understand and be present
For all that stands before me
For all my brothers and sisters
Who help me keep treading on this awfully lonely path.

Yearning

04-08-15

This yearning becomes stronger
If desire is fulfilled it grows
from the physical level to that of heart and spirit
Union engenders the want for more union
Or if thwarted a frustration that must be expressed
through the body
walking in Nature until the heart pounds out its
increasing rhythm
or dancing to the blues until sweat rises to cool the heat

Yet were desire not present
I would not be alive
It is desire that draws us into the world
and the desire for new freedom that finally will draw us out
Or maybe just a deeper peace when our spirits have
grown tired
As I am nowhere near that desire nor remember when I
have been
in another form in another time
I can not speak of it here

Yearning comes for Presence
For communication with Gods and Goddesses
for the sweet respite of the space empty and light or
empty and dark
in meditation
for that moment in orgasm where all is free and unbound
for the ecstasy of dance when effort has released the
endorphins
for those moments when the natural world from the
glowing orb of the the sun
To the short lived burst of a vibrant rainbow or the
overwhelming Being of full moon
captures heart and mind and spirit and there is a sacred pause
Where the breath catches and the heart swells with
wonder and joy

My People

05-02-15

They are the poets whose hearts bleed words
The artists who do not sleep as their Muse drives them home
The blues singers and those who hold the archives to
keep them alive
They are the misguided prophets, the mystics the lost children
of Gods only a little forgotten
They are the lovers
All of these ruled by heart and soul

I am being changed
within and without
To fit a better design
or maybe the original one
Who knows?
I am a slow learner and a late bloomer
But I nurture and nourish this raging passion that rises
from hidden corners and pools the wealth of it long unknown
I welcome it and ask it to change me in its own time
Not too fast or I will break
Nor too slow or I will perish from the longing

I know my sisters and they are legion
They arrive at my doorstep daily in the other world
More numerous than my brothers their comfort is as solid
and as deep as the earth herself
My brothers are fewer, but they come in shining waves
Some are lovers in fact
Some are lovers on another plane but not this one
Some tell me stories to make me heal and laugh
Some make my beauty come forth to greet them
and some teach me to listen and witness their histories
and desires

She is present
I greet Her when I rise and when I venture forth

He is present and gives the strength and healing I need on
the broken days

I am here
I am Priestess
I can and I will carry on

She Who Answers

05-11-15

She who I asked
Has answered me
She who I sought
Has captured me
This sharing of skin and essence
feeds me
Gives me bliss
Changes the current I carry whether conscious of it or
not
There are days where I witness Her in action
Through words I speak
Glances I throw across a room
A way of moving
A way of knowing
That is Hers within mine

So when She interrupts the busy pace
Of a work day
To bid me acknowledge what She has given
How She moves within me and my life
I joyously pick up the pen
Or seek the keyboard
To recognize and deliver the message.

She is whispering
That when we, Her Priest-folk, place limits upon our
thoughts and words
About who we are, and what we are capable of
It is not just a stranglehold on our own capabilities at
the moment
But a barrier to that which She ever so often
and ever so willingly seeks to pass to us and through us
Which is the penetration of Her being within our forms
and lives

A chance to witness the transformation of form to
that which is more essential
That which comes before and after and permeates
Every atom within mass.

Seed Syllable

05-18-15

I don't remember the pain from yesterday so much now
Though I was curled up in a fetal position with the headache
And only 45 minutes to go until the ritual that I do
every month
Dark of the moon
Aware of the foundation that it has established
I lay on the bed curled up and accepting that if Reiki
and pain meds and sinus pills did not work in a timely manner
That I would not be able to do it
Touchstone word here is gratitude

Five minutes before 8pm
I woke up from a doze and carefully moved quickly
Managing with so much help to beat the clock
And be ready on time
In so many ways the ritual was more powerful
Though I was not physically at my best by a long shot
my heart was in my words and the
Presence of the Gods cut through more clearly
Because my need for it had been so profound
Even the divination which can sometimes be muddy
Was spot on.

It had been a day of exhaustion
With crazy sleep patterns and careening energies
As had been the case of most of the week before
Sometimes I ride the wave
Sometimes I am hanging on its edge when it crashes on
the shore
Sometimes my shadow comes out to play and wreaks a
little more havoc
When I am seeking peace instead
All of the above was true
Touchstone word here is strength within vulnerability

The conversations I had with two of the men dearest
to me
Were like standing naked in a windstorm
Vulnerable, open and carrying the courage only the Heart
can manage
New understandings were reached, new accord
New harmonies sounded in the physical and all the other levels
The Lady of Love has shown me such tenderness this year
I bloom within in a way I have hungered for a whole lifetime
Touchstone words here are Love and dedication

Mistress of Love

05-20-15

Part of me was shaking inside even two days later
and not until I was still and quiet in my bed last night
Did I understand the cause
Or maybe it was this morning
You had taken me across a threshold past
The mortal wound left by my prior lover

Lady, you know
the cruelest thing one of us can do to another
Is to allow and encourage the unconditional love that is
our true nature, to draw it out,
Only to conclude an affair letting their lover know they
had been played
and used
Without true regard or respect, let alone love

After a three-year affair with the resulting devastation
I feared that the finest part of me had shut down for
good
In order to heal walls that I had blown down with
purpose
I re-established them the same way
Building a little fortress around my tender heart
Because I had to have a safe space to take the time to
acknowledge
the truth and heal

So with the new moon this past weekend
With two different lovers, I let those walls tumble
or more accurately You led to that threshold
and told me to take the few steps necessary to provoke
the tumbling
Like the game where you stack blocks and keep pulling
out pieces
Until one is the catalyst that sends them all flying

A conversation with one
was a trembling baring of the heart
a renegotiation of our terms so to speak
a request for clarity on boundaries
and the nervousness faded into wonder
as my love spoke his heart and we met in the middle
With ease and new understanding

The other breakthrough was as if I were in Your hands
As my love spoke words that turned a key within me
Words of love and passion
As a warrior lays down shield and weapons in surrender
So did the armoring of my body fall away
and I took joy in the complete opening on all levels
As the Taurean tides, Venus ruled, swept my doubts and fears
away
And the Lady and he played me like a lute
Drawing out only the sweetest sounds

Love Is Dangerous #2

05-20-15

In conversation with myself
in controversy
As the heart says Love is bliss
and the heart remembers also Love is dangerous
It will destroy illusions – some think it creates them
But it is the imagination that will do that
Under Desire's beck and call
But Love is dangerous because it
Unlike us much of the time
Is absolutely fearless
and absolutely ruthless
It will destroy everything that is not Love
in an instant without hesitation

This makes it a diamond of a gift
When we do not get in its way
When we are willing and able to surrender to the same degree
If we fully sign on to serve it
It demands everything of us
It demands that we grow enough to be equal to it
It demands that we let go of the refuse of the past
and the fantasies of the future
It demands that we are present here and now
It demands that we see beyond the surface with clear vision
That we know ourselves and others
That we take care
and that when it gets hard and we need to work
ourselves
down to the bone to uncover it
That we are open to being vulnerable and brutally honest
Over and over and over again
Until it no longer is even something we notice

We just are Love's servants or in other words
Its Priests and Priestesses

What More Do You Want

05-21-15

What will it take for you to understand
The difference between trying to control everything
To make yourself feel safe
and exercising your free will to navigate the waters
and follow the path of wise choices in the moment?

You lost something this morning
and for a few minutes you lost your mind
you panicked
and then you remembered to reach out for help
To invite and trust it
and then you held the two aspects
panic and trust at the same time
When the words came into your head
«If the Gods are really watching over me»
you found the car key within a minute
Please note that the car key sitting out all night on a
public sidewalk
on the city streets of Oakland
shining in the overnight drizzle
Was a sign for you to record and understand
Sigh.

You held yourself in the joy and gratitude of that
moment
All the way to work
Yet you stand here with doubts and anxiety
once again.

You blame the stars, and the planets
You blame the weather
The traffic
Other people and their moods
Oh child
Take a good hard look inside and sort out the elements
you carry within
Discard those that hamper your love and service
and cultivate the others with diligence and tender care

and once in awhile,
Just once in awhile,
Cut yourself a break
and Let Go.

Love Trumps Need

05-25-15

Love trumps need
love trumps desire
love trumps the vagaries of the times
of time itself
love trumps the only curse of Polyamory
there is not enough time in a day or a week or a month
To love enough or as much or as often as we desire
Since love and desire are wed therein

It's OK
It's OK that today did not bring the accomplishments I wanted
Did not fit in with my plans
Did not dance to my tune or bow to my design
In accepting and embracing what is here and now
Peace trumps frustration
and a new direction approaches
Bidding me choose
choose a path
Pick a card
The Trickster Magician winks at me
All paths lead home he whispers
Some just have more "interesting" detours
Than others
Then plants a kiss upon my lips
That invigorates my whole being

Sometimes it is the very need and unsatisfied point
That generates the fire and the heat and the passion
Which will bring about the next bright flight
From the ashes of disappointment
The launch into the glorious unknown
That feeds the very best yet unborn aspects
of Self
That creates the Priest/Priestess anew
bringing enough change and flexibility
to meld and flow with the bumpy waters
to skim the rocks rather than hit them crashing head on
My hardheadedness has never ever gotten me anywhere
Except when bridled under the yoke of the Warrior

Union

05-30-15

Union
Connection
Integration
The blending of hearts and spirits
Before the fire
United within our purpose
Within our love and dedication
The mystery embraces us
As it notes our willingness
To give of ourselves
To give ourselves up
To the incoming rush
Of the essential warmth
that sustains our lives

Lighting the spark within
as the flame grows
Burns and expands
it embraces us all
Later we will find ourselves
bathing anew in warm waters
In the warm gazes of each other's eyes
Within the sweetness of our words
The boundaries dissolve
and we rest
In the Divine Womb of Being
Remembering who we are
Remembering what we are
As we get a taste
Of what is yet to come

Longing for Release

05-31-15

In times of great growth
the heart can expand more greatly
and then contract again
as issues arise that are the roadblocks to fully loving
I admit I love the bliss and recoil
When I see there is work to be done
But only for a moment
Because the work of becoming conscious
Only brings more love into me and my world

whatever my comfort level may be
I am almost always aware that the Universe has my back
I have a loving community that supports me
and when I remember to ask clearly and with heart
For what I need help is always available
From Those I serve
I may not always get what I want and sometimes that
is good
As I can be superficial and chase after shinies
But the big ball of shiny that is purpose and ultimate desire
I do get to taste enough to keep me going
and who could ask for more?

Being taught more and more that Love really does
conquer all
Bringing out ancient shadows who rub their sleepy eyes
and wonder who turned on the lights
I see that this is the work I signed on for
and with grace and fortitude perhaps I will be fortunate
enough
To help a brother or sister down the road

May that purpose beyond all others be fulfilled
This time around.

Conversation with the Goddess

06-06-15

Lady I am a little sad, and a little frustrated
Because my experience did not live up to my expectations
Already I am laughing at myself just saying that
Because that is not the purpose of ritual
and you already gave me my answer
yet I still need to clear out and sort these emotions
Fatigue, sexual frustration, sadness.

I am sad because I have no control over who I desire
Yet you have told me that you are not disappointed in me
and that is balm to my sorrow
I am tired because you rode me and you rode me well
and exactly as I had asked
You gave me what I could handle and no more than that
for as long as I could handle and no more than that
and that is perfect.
I am sexually frustrated, oh just because.
Because I do not have a lover by my side physically right
here and right now
and sometimes that is the only thing that will satisfy
Speak to me if you will Lady
I know there are lessons here and I am Your Priestess
and Your student before all else

You seek Love and you seek Pleasure
and there is no fault in that
But as you offered and as I desired of you today:
You served as my Priestess
You did that this day with the best of your ability
and I have said that you did not disappoint me
I wonder what is it that you seek beyond that

Sometimes you are like a child
Who goes to play with a toy and cries when it does not
work the way you wanted
But living and loving breathing human beings all on their
own roads of evolution
Is not the same
You will need to draw upon compassion and patience
The time will come when you will need to say that you
are not interested
In a sexual relationship with a particular man
And what I counsel you to do is to remember how
tender a human heart is
Remember how easily yours can be hurt
How easily the fire of passion can singe and burn with pain
If not kindled and placed under the yoke of Higher Wisdom

I have placed you here to have your joy and love and
pleasure
But also to temper your desire with your purpose and will
To Love and serve me in the world
As my Priestess
and really
Are you going to complain that I allowed you to do so
this day
Or are you going to wipe tears of joy from your eyes
That it was so
and that you brought a smile to my face in spite of
your own shortcomings.

Some Days Are Designed For Surrender

06-11-15

There are days that flow like swans gliding across a lake
There are days where the sun shines all day within and without
There are days that are roller coaster rides or ferris
wheels spinning
But some days are designed just to bring about surrender

External challenges clearly reflect internal stress
Disruptive emotions bringing awareness of the shadow
never come at convenient times
Self discussion today did finally bring me to acknowledge
That such work is really valuable
as the day I think I am not a work in progress I am
truly screwed

Mercury just went direct this afternoon
and I felt the wobble everywhere
Communications were off to a ridiculous degree
And in the workplace that is just an extra little bit of trying
Kenaz reversed had prepared me although there are
pockets of being
within me that still surprise me when they arise
" Oh it is you again, haven't seen you for years, guess
you still have some hidey holes"

There were also moments of awesome connection and
understanding
just as a scuba diver must have adequate air to carry
him through
There are interluding graces to keep one afloat
All the Gods and we ourselves know we have limitations
and if all the loose ends fray at once the garment is
destroyed

But that moment when the first line of this poem came
That Moment
When I dropped my defenses before what is
The traffic the delays the being late meeting my sweet
sweet friend
It just was the way things were
The reaction to it was sucked out of the situation
and everything shifted

I almost heard my Friendly God sigh
" Well it took you awhile to get to this point today"

But then a wink and a nod and a flashing smile
fading away with him imitating the Cheshire Cat.

To Give

06-14-15

Just as water will flow in a natural path
from a place of fullness to one of emptiness
Giving flows from a full heart and devoted spirit
in its own time and place as easily
One can be attuned to Spirit and listening receive,
and listening, have that which was given go forward
Without an intent or a choice made
Other than the daily desire to serve out of love

Love demands expression and action
It increases when shared and does not live for long
in a cold and selfish heart
Yet love will stay to heal the broken bits within us
Before it will carve a new path forward
This too is well and good

I have little wisdom except to listen
To cultivate a quiet mind and willing spirit
I know that the Universe gives and receives
Just as I breathe in and out
It is a great gift to me when where I stand
There is a need and the Universe expresses an answer to
that need
Through me

this inflow and outflow first gifted me
when I was introduced and made a fit vessel for Reiki
and learned to get out of the way
as that was the only thing that could dam the flow
In practice I can think of the sun in the center of my being
flowing down through my arms and out my hands
or I can let go and fall back into the well spring that
wants to pour
through me
or I can imagine myself as a clear crystal prism
which Reiki uses as a focal point to greet that same
focal point within" another"

Or on the best occasions I can think of nothing at all
and simply be
In that stream
Gratitude conquering all else

Summer 2015

Interfacing with the Silence

06-20-15

There is a man in my life
A dear friend of mine
Who draws the words from me as the ocean
Draws the flow of the river to its embrace
Such mutual joy for us as we taste the sweetness of
non-effort

The desire to write when in his presence
is born from the triggering of portions of Self
that provide deep refreshment
Always it is as if I have reached an oasis after time in a
barren desert
Yet Silence laughs at me reminding me that it wears
different guises
Most often I am in its embrace in meditation or
powerful Reiki sessions
But only with my friend Ari
Does it intercede itself within and through discourse

It is a rare and precious thing
To experience the Stillness as a familiar ally and
comforting companion
It knows to relax me utterly requires a special flavor of
its vast energy
To draw me to it naturally without any effort except an
attentiveness
Rising from the wonder of my childlike heart center
It opens the channels and arouses my willingness to
venture forth
Into new territory

There is a sweetness to it
and a slightly teasing quality as if it were laughing gently
With one raised eyebrow
As if to say
What took you so long to return here?

And then a giggle
With that release that comes from giggling like the children
Who have not forgotten
How to play with ease and total abandon

There are some amongst us
Who by their Presence
Bring space for Magic to arise
and to be shared

It Gets Stirred

06-22-15

Seasons shift
The wheel turns
That which was fixed and immobile
Breaks into thunderous and sudden movement
That which was stuck gets unstuck

The joy of being with a lover
Leaves tears at their parting
A part of living devoted to work
Suddenly ceases
Friendships shift and groan with stresses
But resolve in better understanding

Passions quicken
And dissolve in the climax
One rides the crest of the wave
To be dropped upon a foreign shore
The ecstasy of the light
Reveals pieces of unhidden shadow
Bliss brings courage within its peace
So that one is able to continue
When in the ruins
Of Satori

And She who holds us all
Stirs the pot and stirs it once again
With Her faces melding one into another
One of fierce compassion
One of bone-breaking Love
One of tender sorrow
One of childlike innocence
And you who witness must hush your breath
As this kaleidoscope of Being
Haunts what is left of your vision

Dog Paddling

06-23-15

So they asked me if I knew how to swim
In these unfamiliar waters
I said I knew how to dog paddle or tread water
But I had only watched others swim, and heard their stories
Or read about swimming
So I sometimes became really nervous

They asked me why I wanted to swim
My reply was that it calls to me
As Love calls to the Lover
As the flower calls to the bee
as the Moon calls to the tides
it is as natural a pull to my spirit as these things
though I have not the experience to make me feel
secure in the water
Yet

Then I looked around and I saw you
With your swimmer's body
and your magnetic eyes
and you did not laugh when I was clumsy
or uncomfortable with the newness of doing actual swimming
even though I still reverted to treading water at times
You showed me how to gradually with patience and ease
Make the necessary transitions
one by one

Show Me Your Hidden Face

06-26-15

This dance we do
From strangers, slowly and tenderly perhaps to intimates
Is more intoxicating than the finest wine.
My overture to you – when after months
My thoughts were drawn once again to you,
More intensely than at the beginning,
When I knew that it was youthful inexperience that sought
To make you conform to a pattern that had nothing to do with you,
Nor your will nor your heart nor you own dance between love and attachment
And freedom –
I realized only that had driven a wedge between us.
Love laughed and said why not try again

So I wrote you and when you told me
Face to face that you never read your emails
(I had forgotten)
I spoke the same words to you then.
As boldness overcame fear and shyness
" I miss you,
I miss your humor and your compassion,
I miss the peace bomb you dropped on me as I lay sleeping
I want to begin again"

I expected nothing and gave all that I had in that moment.
I forgot what everybody said when they said you gave only to the music.
I desired nothing in that moment but to let Love greet you through me.

The gift that you gave was the walls tumbling,
You let me in.
You showed me your hidden face
You triggered the release of mine
And we have begun again
To play with one another
To laugh and to flirt and to let the music
Lead us where it will

When you ask me to come back and see you again soon
There is a part of me as vulnerable as you
That quivers in resonance and smiles
As I respond, of course
As soon as I can

She Dances

07-04-15

She dances through the currents
of a sea deeper than any ocean known by man
She dances in the stars of a heaven vaster than the
finest instruments
Can begin to map
She reaches us from the deepest parts of us, primal
and not possible
To be consciously known
and She speaks

Why do you live in fear, still, my children
When you are tested, does it not bring forth the best in you?
When I have stripped you down
Freeing you from your obsessions, those desires not
worthy of you
your desire for control, your desire to be the top of the
shit pile
Can you not know that your deepest want is to drink at
my fountain
That which carries the healing waters of love,
understanding and forgiveness
As well as that salty touch of instigation
That desire to provoke and prod and stir things up
But in My name, not your own

Sometimes I lose patience
because We have not made stupid children
Yet your desire to use your free will without partnering
it with the
Wisdom of the heart and spirit and body
Is a crime against everything that lives in the world you share
As is evident in the mess you have collectively made of things

Open your eyes and see what your carelessness has wrought
The earth cries in pain
You are wiping out living species faster than I can
create new ones
Unless I blow up the whole thing and start over completely
And that is not My desire at this time
With your infinite capacity for Love as your birthright
Why oh why do you seek out to find your capacity for Egotism
Cruelty and Competition
You appear to race to your own destruction more often
than not

Yet there is that within you that is astounding in its beauty
Powerful in its Love and determination
Tender in its care of all your relations and yourselves
Had I not seen it growing in the wreckage of these days
of shifting
I would not still be here to give you good counsel

Ease up your ways racing to pile up goods or money or fame
Or power
Ease into a rhythm that speaks to your breath and body
a natural way that blends with the ways of the Earth
the Stars the Sun and the Moon
Your teachers are all around you
There is not one moment in one day that one will not
respond to you
If you put the call out
But you must be still enough to hear their answer
Change how you live to harmonize with your true nature
Keep it simple
Your resources on this planet are not without limit
Manage what you have
We watch to see whether you will grow up enough
To continue on
Or whether you will fail as an evolutionary experiment

I am hedging my bets in your favor
But you had better light that fire within you
and make good on the promises made to Me
in the in between time
Before it is too late

You Cannot Run From Your Own Heart

07-18-15

You can't run and you can't hide
You can try and tell yourself a lie
You can hide beneath the covers
You can think about other lovers
But the heart knows its own secrets
and nothing will stand in its way

You can get entangled and triggered in old wounds
They can wrap their sticky webs about you
But the signal the heart sends never waivers
Open and see
It will repeat this louder and louder
In your waking hours and in your sleep
It will torment you and show you its pain
from being forcibly closed
Until you break and surrender to its opening again

In that moment the pain stops
In that reaching out for the one you love
In the willingness to acknowledge your missteps
Your panic at the thought of not being loved which in truth
is the panic at not Being Love
Which is the Biggest Lie of all
It is impossible to not be what you are

Waves of gratitude bathe me
Escape happened
Escape happened from the trap of thoughts of lack
Escape happened from blocks within me to hearing
another's voice
To knowing from inside what their world was looking like
at that moment
That I was stuck only seeing my own wants and needs
Perspective was given

and a warning from the Sage known as the Iching
That made me grab my writing tool
and reach out from the broken place
With all that I am
So that healing could begin
Within myself
and therefore between us

The Need to be Fluid

07-25-15

I watch the dust settle and reflect
on what is left after things shake out
On how extremes in stress can be received
and that the damages show where tools need to be
honed and used
More often

The last moon has carried changes powerful to
bring out the Shadow and bring out the Strength and Love
In their dance together sometimes one was on top and
then the other
But it was the intensity that brought me tumbling down
It built until one day, walking for my sanity I acknowledged
to Those who listen and hear
That I had been taken past the point that I could bear
and I just let go

My desire to have any particular result was decimated
Only one desire left
That for peace and the degree of balance and sanity
Needed to keep me going
Nothing mattered except that stability found from the
deepest access point
to Self and to the Heart wherein everything else exists
I sought only the Presence of the moment
and Yes
I needed to submerge myself within it utterly and
completely
That which survived within which was central and the
experience of it was
all that I needed to recognize and cultivate

I recognized that too much stress had made me negative
and chose to correct that immediately
no matter what was impacting my body mind and spirit
from external circumstances
I took back my power to be what and whom I choose
to be in this world
I took back the Priestess
I took back Service to the whole as my prime directive
I took back Love as my wellspring
and I made a stand at that moment in the middle of
another mad day at work
I took back my life

I am not for sale nor will I rent space in my head
for the madness that surrounds me in this world
I know that I hold my own piece of madness
as well
I will not cultivate it nor focus on it other than in
acceptance
I carry the Remedy
It is given me each and every day through the medicine of
Practice
Of Devotion, and those Allies human and Other, who
bring me Joy

Thinking of You

08-11-15

Like the days of summer
Golden in their light and easy in their manner
Or those moments in life where the world's stress
Vanishes within the larger framework
Your presence is a healing balm

The music helps
But the music is a medium for what you are
communicating energetically
The signals I read are a combination of your signature in
and of itself
And the expression of it through dance and music
Provoking within me both peace and heat
Truly a potent and rare combination in my experience
But one that brings me joy, and happiness and love

You remind me of those days long ago when I thought
my generation
Would change the world
And on some levels we absolutely did
Though you have to go deep and wide to see that,
unless you still carry that energy.
We were naïve and we were innocent
But we were betting everything on Heart and Spirit
I still do and will for as long as I am here
As do you.

You are a gift to my life
The parameters no longer matter to me
Though my desire may slip through on occasion
To touch in physicality
But whatever it takes to make you happy
Whatever boundaries enable you to keep the peace within
While functioning in the outer world
Keep them darling

I do not want you to change a thing
As we meld in the way we meld
My joy increases

Just know along with everything else
To keep the vernacular simple and not crude
You also make my toes curl

Altar of Love

08-12-15

I am an altar of Love
This body Her playground
This flesh when fully permeated with Her presence
becomes luminous and light and beautiful
Beyond the normal
The heart surrenders to the expansion and opens fully
To receive
To listen and learn
As Her whispers guide and tantalize

In those moments I live
I have been broken open too much for anything less
To satisfy
I take delight in any service I can give Her
Anytime and anything that can draw Her more completely into
This world
I call it Priestess work
She laughs and says
"You call it work?"
I laugh with Her, as there is no hardship in it
Only Bliss

I reflected today on the four men in my life that I adore
Three only touch me through cyberspace
Sacred space dependent on careful reading of energy,
more so even than here
and the Gods have been thoroughly illustrating that all worlds
are One world

One is in my vicinity, and S is the most mysterious in
his place in my life
Perhaps his is the most complex and demanding role
Yet also the most tangible when we are able to meet
face to face
Priest he is, and answered my call
Yet a lover of many, as he too serves Her before all else

My brother A who lives in the silence, the purest
empath I have ever met
Greeted me when we first met as if I was a long lost
twin of his
Touching him is to still everything and just listen and be.
He is balm to my spirit and mind and together we are
more than separate
we bathe in those calm perfectly still waters whenever we can
Both rejuvenated by our visit and touched by Spirit

The one who is of my generation, P
Enthralls me with his knowledge and love of Music
I believe that She is his Mistress
As he spends more time preparing for his work as a DJ
than anything else
and has more knowledge of the blues than anyone I have
ever met
Again we touch only in cyberspace and the in between
But his energy is an enticing mix of passion and heat
Self-containment and deep peace
I do not know exactly what draws him to me
Except that I am totally willing to love him and take him
as he is
He is the man with the fiercest boundaries
Yet he has honored me by letting me in
and that has carved out a place only for him
in my softening heart

Last but not least is my friend, B
Who is also my lover
My counselor
my companion
I have no secrets from him
and trust him utterly with my naked bare heart
He has seen me fall apart
and seen me light up like a Christmas tree
and everything in between
His role is to listen and accept
Which has been the greatest gift
For my own self acceptance and self esteem

When I have said that this was the happiest year of my life
It is because I have know Her better
Experienced that tiny trickle of the pure Love that She IS
To the degree that this human/divine hybrid is capable
I have met and loved more people than ever except maybe
in those
turning points of a lifetime
The sixties
the late eighties
the early twenties(LOL) and the Ecstasy and Agony of
2012 when everything changed
there are crossroads where the Grace Waves come and
knock me on my ass
only to fling me into a free fall where I can take pure
joy in living

This year has opened the doors for my next adventure
and Love in Her full Dignity, beckons me take each step
Without fear and with devotion
Leaving the rest up to Her.

You Thrill Me

08-17-15

Hot, worn out, and tired, balking at work
My thoughts still travel towards you
Perhaps you draw me like a magnet
Because being around you just brings me joy
I don't know what it is about you
Especially since what pulls so powerfully is behind the
curtain so to speak
It is the energy of you
Since the form you have chosen in our strange alternate
universe
Can only serve as a conduit for the man who lives behind it

From the first time I saw you
There was a taste of the full tilt boogie thrill I have
now
I would say that by the time you peace bombed me in
the sweet deep darkness of the night
I was a goner without even knowing it
Like an adolescent girl I was knocked off balance
and chased you till I embarrassed myself
and then ran away

Though that aspect of me had to be retired to the
distant past where girls rule
The wisdom of the Priestess who is embodied in the
disguise I wear in our shared world
came to my rescue
I do not regret the mistake because it provided the
space for the return
I grew up a little and recognized that I wanted you
within your terms and boundaries
and that the value of you to me was a whole lot deeper
than your pretty face
and skill with music, or even the heat that you awaken
so well

Because just as a musician can work a crowd and bring
healing through his magic
You perform the same service of healing on a very deep level

I have no desire to run away
My only hindrances to the complete immersion in the joy
of our time together
are the ideas that Love cannot live outside of all the
commonly accepted boxes
Yet I have found more transformation and growth in the
eight months in SL
than in the last three or four years in RL
You are a treasure to me - I would not trade you for
any other
I will take the longings that cannot be fulfilled
the desires that must be sublimated
the fires that burn hotter each time we connect
and that taste of you in the dark when you visit and
wake me
and adore the whole package
You revitalize me

I will neither walk nor run away this time
I will revel in my heart's delight in you.
Just as I revel in yours for me.

Depression

08-19-15

It as if a monster has awoken to tear me to pieces
But not from outside, though the social anxiety of
the night before, and worries about close relationships
triggered it
This one rises from deep inside where my secrets lie
My deepest insecurity and deepest loneliness and isolation
These are its weapons
It draws its sharp claws down my inner heart, shredding
me as it goes
and it sings its song to me:

" No one loves you
You are alone and will always be alone
You are a failure in your relationships
You cannot take care of yourself
You will be poor and unwanted and old
You are no longer attractive
No one wants you
Your days are numbered"

Whew!
between last night and this morning it has struck me
I have curled into a fetal position, even in my sleep
and wake up wondering how I will get through the day
I do my practice and ask for strength to gird myself for
this old battle
Fought many times, though less than when I was younger
I rejoice that Wednesday always brings me extra joy and
strength
Because of special offerings to Odin and Hermes

I gratefully place one of Odin's talismanic necklaces
upon my neck
and dress in a joyous color of turquoise
I am strengthened by these actions
Even if I am still bleeding inside

On the ride to work, again heavily laden with daily
practice
Prayers and affirmations and healing work for self and
others
When it interfered to say
" No one loves you"

A strong voice rose from within
" I Love Me"

and for once in my life I knew it to be true
and it was enough for now

The Night Before

08-22-15

She calls me to Her side and says
"Sit here next to me for awhile and let us talk about love
and magic and what makes them light up and what
quenches their fires"
"What are you beginning to learn?"

The fires burn as they will
In their own time and all my yearning still
does not make them come nor burn higher
But releasing my expectations and fears
My grasping and my greed
and simply opening and trusting their power and their
compassion
while resting myself in Your arms
frees both them and me and whomever I am loving at
that time

Not making up stories certainly will help
Not presuming to know what a lover feels
Nor what may be keeping him away or making him
unavailable
in presence or emotionally
Being sensitive to everything around me and not just my
own internal state
and knowing all the ways to self love and to give of myself
in ways where You lead me that do not involve
One of my heartrendingly beautiful crushes

and there is another secret Mama
and that is to welcome the bonfire
to welcome the cracking open of the heart
The vulnerability the tenderness and surrender
To welcome the journey
The rush of the waters that carry me away
just as much as the return and the cessation of passion
The firmness of the ground under my feet
The peace of the still mind

Oh but Mama
You know of all Beings
How brightly they burn
My brothers of the Light
Their Spirits and Their Wills
Their Gilded Hearts
and Their well conquered Minds

You know of all Beings
Why I am helpless to do anything but
Adore them
As they are Your sons
Just as I am Your daughter

Branded by Longing

08-27-15

From out of nowhere the thought of you comes
And with it the memory of the few tokens of our exchanges
Your voice
Your sometimes cryptic comments
Your heart which you guard and expose unexpectedly
Your mastery of the music you present

Blindsided, as I am at work
Simply trying to carry on under less than ideal conditions
and what, I ask, am I to do with this longing for you
So far away
So inaccessible except within your tightly prescribed
boundaries

The Lady laughs
" What do you usually do?"
She asks
I burn, Lady
I pour gasoline on that fire that the longing brings
Whether I burn alone, or with another
the burning is the only thing that satisfies the longing
Within this immolation, the heart bursts open
and the constriction of desire unfulfilled goes up in smoke
With the release of it and the joy of being consumed
once again.

Love Simultaneous

09-04-15

I sit trembling as my heart expands
for in this moment it is full to capacity of love for two men
Aflame in an upward and outward rush of heat and passion
With a depth that reaches as far inward and to the root
of it all
I know that I am in it now, and in for it
and I tremble once again
as the earth must feel when she shakes
Because there is no turning back from this call
no more than a moth can resist the beckoning of its
own demise

Burn baby, burn
Burn off the hesitation and fear
the misshapen ideas of yesterday and last year's model
of Self
trade it in for a better model
This journey has just begun
The first step barely taken
There is something feral in the Lady's gaze as Her eyes
bore into me
Come, She says, I have what you have been seeking
What you have been asking for

You have asked for your freedom
Come see, I hold it here in my hand
It will feel like having wings to fly
and all you need is to take a deep breath and release everything
that holds you down
you may keep your roots in the heart of the earth
But you may not let the world hold you captive

Tell me again what your song was earlier today, Daughter

I will not be bound by the small mindedness of men
Nor enslaved by their evil
I will seek the wild ways, the ways of earth tribes
whose ancient song rises from the
stones
I will find them though their palaces and temples may
be in ruins
I will taste the energy of the Gods and Goddesses
That these fools courting death have tried to destroy
I will put all that I have on the line for Them
My heart, my spirit, my mind and my will
I will not ever be a slave again
I would court Death before I succumb to the
dominion of those who have sold
themselves
For power and lies
This time around will count and has been given over to You
that I served long before this day.

Opened By a Handful
of Loving Words

09-08-15

the word is flow
the word is surrender
the words are making love
love is creating the words
and the space between us is not
two states away
but here
right here and right now

with a few words and your pure intent
you zeroed in and let your arrow fly
and it struck in the middle of my heart
and everything became still
as I felt my heart welcome that arrow
and wrap itself around the message it carried
this was the second very major surprise and imprint that
you left

Actually the third on your instigation and one on mine

The first was the comment you made in the club
about me being a mobile wet spot
Those words stopped me in my tracks
and though I did not know it at the time
we began

The second was the peace bomb
which woke me just to leave me drenched in the deepest peace
I had ever felt

The third was the conversation we had where I acknowledged and
seconded by intent the desire that Love have its way with us
In its finest most unselfish perfection

The fourth was tonight
when you said you would watch over me
the world stopped
my heart opened completely
I felt a kind of safety that is rare for me

and then, being who I am
Asked if I could write...

Climbing Trees

09-10-15

When I was a girl I loved to climb
the grapefruit trees on our rental property
Climb to a different vantage point and contemplate hidden there
I loved to ride my bicycle on the flats
as far as my legs would carry me
I had freedom and could follow my desires

These days desire awakens yet I can not gratify it
except in the midnight fantasies and even then
I have neither face nor form that connects to the man
you are
Behind the curtain
Only the sweet fine taste of your energies

I want to climb you like my favorite tree
Slide down and plant myself firmly on your branch
rest there awhile until movement is demanded
listen to the stillness and watch as our energies blend
and that which is us rather than you and I
Reveals another layer

I want to ride you like I rode my bike
legs pumping and breath deep
pushing to my limits as you fill me
Opening to receive you as far as you want to go
testing first my limits and then seeing if I can find ours

Today on my walk I thought of you and this poem rose up
I felt the vitality of that young girl, perhaps ten
and I knew myself in her and her in me
I am still here
I am still vital
I am more capable than ever of giving of myself
As this journey has led me to love myself

Maybe I will send this to you and
maybe I will find that just as it makes me blush
(who knew I still can)
I will chicken out
because other than tasting and blending our energies at
the club
I have no knowledge of your sexuality nor your desire

Perhaps I never will
But I can still share my own
If you are a willing audience
I will not make you a captive one...

Waking Up

09-11-15

This unexpected resurgence of desire
makes me tumble and stumble over myself
Standing at my workstation
my root and second chakras humming like a beehive
Are distracting
All day I have been endeavoring to focus on work
First my thoughts kept moving to you
When I managed to corral them
The body chimed in

There is good stuff happening with paradigm shifts
regarding relationships here
at some point I had enough damages that falling for someone
(Even though I am innately very trusting of you in particular)
made me feel like I was walking into an emotional minefield
With the exception of a twelve-year marriage
Loving has not been safe nor conducive to good self-esteem
or unconditional loving

If there was a broken part of my life it was in the
companionship I sought
and I took solace in amazing friends,
Became accustomed to celibacy and long periods of loneliness
an expert at sublimation.

I love that you do not fit into any model
You do not resemble anyone else in my life
Though I would not be surprised if somewhere in the
place where
we draw our ideals
there is a template that looks something like you
To be caught off guard and surprised by you day by day
Without feeling like there should be a safety net
underneath me
Has left me with a smile on my face much of the time
and a hunger to spend all the time possible with you

Where have you come from, my darling one?

Blue Song

09-14-15

The day was relaxed
Time spent with friends
one on one
and a poetry reading in the early evening
where I was surprised and honored to win the evening's prize
always a little awkward at being in the spotlight
My poems are a gift and just pass through me to the paper
Them, I can shine a light on happily
Me, I have lived observing on the sidelines for too long

I went to another blues club
To hear my sister work her magic
I have oodles of feminine support there
and normally it energizes and comforts me
But I was down, depressed and deeply blue
My heart was so close to the surface
Every love song sang to me
and the longing was upon me
I knew there was only one cause

This was a night when I would not see you

Made no difference that I saw you on Friday
and on Saturday
That I drank my fill of your energies and gave
As good as I got
Sunday was not going to hold that joy

I had a chat with a fellow poet
and he was smart and witty and quite sweet
and I enjoyed it and we accepted the possibility of
friendship

Then I went to my bed and all was about you

when I dipped my toes in the water
following my heart
and swam to you
I did not know these currents would run so deep
nor that I would welcome them while trembling at their
ability to open me so wide

What Longing do the Angels Harbor?

09-15-15

Sunlight blazing from a clear blue sky
touching this tired body
tired heart

tired of the age old battle between surrender
to Love alone
and desire
there is a point where I even tire of desire
Because it burns
yet consumes me not
it provokes
yet does not satisfy
It claims its territory with longing
the only thing more powerful than my desire for freedom
is my desire to merge
to taste
to know, to fully experience
That which tantalizes me so

Today I wanted to ask you for five minutes a day
where I could hear your voice on the phone
But feared I had no right
That trigger was instituted by the unrehearsed unplanned
Laugh that happened the other night
at the club
it was like sexy velvet and perfect masculine joy
I wanted to rub my ears in the sound like a cat
rubs against your ankles
and of course voice to voice connection is delicious
I have no siren call nor desire to remove any bricks in
your walls
Though if the mortar weakens and you allow me leeway
I will proceed with tender care

Writing to you this way is the only time
I can freely touch on the territory within my heart
where I invited you to establish residence
It is the only way I can be active in expressing how I
really feel
about you
without the distractions we are under
worrying about messing with your work
or struggling with my own frustration
Because I am helpless in my desire
to know you
to touch you
to speak and listen
to take walks

I miss the visits you would make in the deep of night

Angels fly as birds do
Each in love with light and sky and the movement of the wind
I fly to you with words
Praying that you receive them in the spirit they are given,
with joy of your own

Love's Feast

09-16-15

Love nibbled on me for breakfast
Chomped away at me for lunch
and down right devoured me for dinner

"Tastes Good" Love said
mmmm
"Good taste," said I

Love tickled my ribs and
I collapsed on the floor laughing
"What took you so long?" I asked,
breathless,
"What took you so long to be ready to receive me?"
Love answered in a sweet and tender tone

Love pondered quietly while giving me the eye
"You are what they call a late bloomer
and I know that you hated that, but do you have any
complaints for me now?"

Tipping my head saucily, I winked at Love and bowed deeply
"none whatsoever dear Love, I know you have many more
tricks up your sleeve.
tricks to open me wider drop me deeper blur all my
boundaries until in relief I see them for what they are.
imaginary strands of cobweb waiting to be blown away
like dandelions"

Love gave me a deep and serious and considering look:
"Are you telling me you are completely ready for the ride
of your life?"

I answered humbly and just as seriously
"Oh Love, I do not know if I am ready or not, but I
know that if you do not take me fully and completely,
Inside and out, with every shape and taste and touch and
sound and scent permeated by your presence,
I will most certainly die from longing for you"

Love smiled, winked, took off His/Her hat
and with a Cheshire smile faded back into the Light.

Yes, My Love

09-18-15

you bring the best of me to the surface
As it pushes through and out
I am learning to let it be
To let the heart unfold as it will
Precious few opportunities in life for it to be
as open as it will and feel safe enough
to open more
Because you receive me with grace

These words are shaped by this opening
which slides down my body and opens all the energy centers
and I breathe in the joy of this
the joy of having you in my life
the joy of touching as we do
and there is no denying that we do

What you teach me is to live in the now
To put a halter and a lead on a mind that is not firmly
anchored in it
I can have the joy and love and deep peace of the now
or watch it run around in circles of what ifs and whens
and maybes
More and more I just don't care about the futility of
those thought patterns
there is no comparison to what you present to me when
we come together

You excite me
you get my levels humming and buzzing and you are all
they talk about
In the middle of the day
at work
driving fully focused on doing that well
when the music is playing
when I am walking
I think of you and I feel you
and you make my life sweeter and richer for it

thank you baby
whatever unfolds between us
I wait for the next movement
and all I can do is smile
with my whole Being

Walking in Accord

09-20-15

Under the shelter of the heavens
I have no fear
Step by step I follow the winding mountain trail
from the profound comfort of the long tall standing people
on the lower levels
You take me to the less traveled and more barren heights
Where the winds have scoured the vegetation clean
Except for those hardy ones which still hang on
as if part of the rock itself

Even the streams which had gladdened my journey below
are no longer visible
No spring hidden in a lush corner pocket
Tucked away until the thirsty traveler stumbles upon it
You have led me to these lonely parts for a purpose

The struggles and exhaustion felt at the beginning
As my body adjusted to elevation and muscle fatigue
have been stripped away
As I look from this vantage point
You show me a vista deep and wide and far-reaching
Clouds drifting across it carrying the dance of shadow
and light
Why am I here, I ask?

To get you unstuck
You answer
To show you once again that wrestling with yourself is
poor sport
Seek the stillness and lay down the willful ways of a child
Always seeking pleasure and satisfaction
Always seeking some certain answer to what the future holds

Dance with me on this peak
Throw off the nonsense you let fill your pretty little head
Have I not shaped you with care these many years
Let you observe and hear the secrets whispered on the wind
When will you be satisfied with the ways of living I
have ingrained in you
and simply let the flow of moment to moment
take you aware but completely relaxed
Where the next calling beckons

Fall
2015

Aftermath of Ritual

09-21-15

The day set the tone from the first awakening
Hardly up at all and the poem came
From my patron deity
Who in his direct but gentle way
Guided me to clarity regarding the bits making me feel stuck
Since the working was with His wrathful aspect
To clear obstacles
Such clarity was priceless

One forgets the stamina demanded
When one is captured within the structure of a long
Theurgic working
Well attuned to each other though I have not been active
In the Order for at least five years
We were both receivers and transmitters
in this connecting with Hermes Pantos Apolytos
The All-Liberating Aspect of Him

Once before I had done this ritual,
But with a smaller group
Though I remembered much of it and stumbled less
A tongue not toned to do the 108 repetitions of mantra
after mantra
Still stumbled more than I would have liked
Yet what I will call my perception muscle is better

There were some new ingredients thrown in
One was that three alchemical tinctures brought in
Before we started
Amazed at their effectiveness
I was grateful for the aid and the skillful means my
comrades provide
In addition, I found out later than my friend who does
Radionics had linked
To two people not present, which gave me a new window
into what is possible with that
Modality

At a certain point when the energies were built quite high
I was led to send to two of the three men who I adore
the third was present
My heart is full knowing each of them
and what prompted me to write this poem
Was at least partially the understanding that though I
may be truly frustrated
That I cannot meet these two in the here and now
physically
There is so much that I know is possible outside of that
Whether it is expressed in ritual connecting with a
particular Deity
Or loving and communicating with someone in SL

A major working for me these days is silencing the parts
of me
Who squawk about what is lacking in my life
When I am rich in experiences that bring me joy and
satisfaction
I have always thought the cup half full to overflowing
For some reason, there has been struggle the last
couple of years
With an unwanted half empty persona arising.

I will find the cure for that.

The Enemy Within

09-23-15

You arrive at the most inconvenient times
In the midst of making love with words
You thrust your ideas in
Insecurity, fear, embarrassment
As if I have no reason to be alive
Or the work done and dues paid were to no avail
You sit smirking from your dark corner
Trying to convince me that my love is all lies

and sometimes you work on me and I believe you
for five minutes

Then, thank Goddess, I have the history of my life
I can see when I began to become free from your
coercion
when I started to emerge as Priestess and Lover
when I started to care more about others and less
about my small self
when transformation and the Gods reached towards me
and I towards Them
Until the connection became so clear that doubt cannot
arise about THAT again

So yes
In a new love affair, there are old insecurities triggered
Self-doubt has a small corner
a lack of confidence an inch or two
But my trump card is that I will throw away my lust
for results
over and over until there is not a fragment of it left
No matter how long it takes this will be done
and without that you have no foothold
Because I am not invested in a particular future
I only want to be with my feet deeply immersed
in the stream of Being
with fear washed away as I submerge myself in Love

Love freely given
will be received as such
and will grow

Love freely accepted
will grow
and be shared exponentially

Love cannot be bound nor polluted.
In its tender arms
neither can I.

I've Been Listening

09-24-15 pm

Listening and watching
The skies with their paint brush clouds swirling
through
That perfect clear vision blue
striking me with awe
Felt familiar
As this is the time of year I love to feel the wheel turn
and the change of the season

Driving home there were great patches of stillness
You were on my mind
I thought of all the times our connection has been
crystal clear
with a pristine awareness
That being crazy about you
Is the sanest thing that has ever happened to me

The deeper I go in contemplation of this thing we have
between us
The deeper my joy at your presence in my life
You wake up the healthiest parts of me
and they are all standing at attention
I am moved to not miss a second
To go full out to go full in
With all the intensity I can muster
Because you deserve all the good stuff I got to give

I have a sense sometimes of what a good man you are
Beyond the heat
There is the warmth of your being, your heart
Behind the persona that fits your environment and your
service to your passion
there is a wisdom coupled with an intelligence that loves
to teach
Behind the wise cracking, a sweetness of nature
that brushes against me sometimes making me shiver
with the still beauty of it

That you should care for me
heals and crumbles old stuff that just is not necessary
any more
your presence in my life rejuvenates my spirit
and frees my vision of myself
from what anybody else thinks of me
including sometimes myself

I like the version of me that comes out to play with you
Given the opportunity you will see more and more of her
as she lightens up and comes to the forefront

I am totally grateful for the man I have come to know.

I Have This Feeling

09-29-15

I have this feeling
when I open to that which moves between us
that we will never be boring
at least not to each other
that your intellect and your passion
will meet mine in harmony
and escalation
as long as we come together

I have this feeling
that I will be entranced by your depths
those qualities that support your being
but are not on the surface
those traits of yours that tantalize me
the abilities and freedom that challenge me
to kick off self-imposed limitations
and deny those I have allowed others to fetter me with
as long as we come together

there is more:
since I was a very young woman
I have known that the path of sex
at least in this lifetime
Is a spiritual path for me
as well as a thrill that has not lost its edge but
sharpened over the years
I have found it impossible to find my match
in exploring where these paths meld
and all that is possible
I know there are places we could go
if we choose to do so
Which would satisfy that longing
as long as we come together

There is so much wealth in that primal drive
That so few even begin to taste

I yearn to go there with you.

Bliss Like Thunder
and Lightning

10-02-15

after a night with dozing and dreaming
and no remembrance of deep sleep
I stumbled out of bed and was dizzy with my ears plugged
from the parting sinus infection
and struggled and worked with every trick I could come
up with and
Lots of appealing for help
Which finally got me in the car and on my way
Though being stuck on street parking took a lot of defrost

On the walk I was oppressed by a foreboding of an
unknown source
Which finally resulted in me seeking protection
I warded myself and appealed to 4 Gods who are my
Guardians
and the Goddess whose talisman I wore –
by the time I was nearly back at the office
it had eased and in gratitude I dealt with a strange day

Instead of the stressful meltdown of the last few months
Obstacles were removed in interesting ways
Such as the other half of my job paying vendors was
put on hold
Stuffed myself with lunch and then administered
caffeine to stay awake
Got done and out the door an hour after normal quitting time
Which gave me such a taste of freedom as to blow off
stress with ease

The Friday night traffic jam with the bridge work
compounding it
Made it slow going
But
The first taste of Bliss power came upon me as I sat
and grew still and the moment rose with the thought
It does not matter where you are or what you are doing
This moment contains it all
The bliss came upon me and shook me
I panted and hyperventilated as it had its way with me

The aftermath was a core strengthening that got me
home
without any fatigue

lit Loki's candle and incense for Those Displaced and
Welcomed
then left the room to fiddle around with costuming for Aqua

Laid down to take a nap so I could have my precious
time in the club tonight later
read a little and closed my eyes
Only to have the bliss slam into me again
but from the root up – several times shook me out of
all thoughts of a nap

Gonna have a cup of tea and welcome what the nighttime
brings

What Does It Mean—
I Can Count On You

10-04-15

This phrase came up today in conversation with my brother
as I struggle off and on with insecurity
and I acknowledged that I can count on him and a
mutual friend of ours
Which triggered the desire to dig
So I have gotten my shovel
and I am gonna break it down

I can count on you
Reduce that to its raw form
I want to be able to count on my friends and my lovers
To always love me
I want to count on myself to always love them back
and deeper yet
I don't want our relationships to change or to end
which begs the question
How much of my happiness am I betting on that

Being crazy in love is not the same as unconditional loving
which I find much easier with friends or lovers with
strong boundaries
Defining what is to be given and received on each person's part
a map, so to speak that gives some structure to what
we are engaged in
what we each want and need
and what we want to nurture and grow between us

So this element of uncertainty is not JUST due to fear
of losing love
or self-esteem issues

Some of it is because I am engaged in a wholly
undefined relationship
the only solid thing that I can count on
Is the call of my own heart to you
and your welcome response to me when I get there

This feels like Love is demanding me to be some kind of
grown up
Which leaves me at times kicking and screaming like a
little girl
afraid somebody or something is gonna take her candy away
The strength of me is within the woman and the
Priestess
Neither of whom are gonna walk away from this one
and with those words both heat and Love rise up within me
and once again I surrender to the moment in its perfection
and let fear dissolve.
I also just realized, that as I entrust these words into
your care
When you pick up this poem later
Being able to get this real and raw with you –
That truly is counting on you in a very special way.

You Want A Guarantee

10-04-15

So you have pinged Me
and have waited all day for an answer which I will give you
You did the work to be honest with yourself
and it is time now for you to listen to the answer

You want a guarantee of being loved
Of having results because your heart is involved
Which means you miss the point completely
The gift you have been given is that your heart is involved
Utterly and completely and deeply
It is opening and shows no signs of closing
and yet you tell me that this terrifies you

I am giving you a taste of what living fully will mean
and yes it means no holding back
Giving everything because it feels better than anything in
human experience to do that
and yes you will feel vulnerable
and you will not know what is going to happen next
and the taste of freedom will be sweet in your mouth
and you will not be so hungry for one man to love you
Because Love will have torn you open and taken you captive
and Joy will be your birthright

You are My Priestess
You are not a sniveling child
You are not at the mercy of the emotions of any other person
male or female
You are not dependent on their good graces
Or them seeing you
Or knowing you to be who you are meant to be

That is the trap you keep falling in
Yet have I not sent you always at least one person
Who knew and cared for you
at the very least – your whole life – one friend

You have such support in the human community
and if you have any doubt about Us
Then you have not been paying any attention at all to
your own life

I have said this before and I say it again now
You are your only enemy, your only roadblock your only carrier
of fear and limitation
Step forward and take the reins for your own wild horse self
The future is open and Love ever present.

Take My Heart

10-05-15

Take my heart
Make it pliable, open and receptive
able to flow with its inherent nature of
Unconditional Love
Make it fluid and resilient
Let it be the strongest voice in my being
Let it penetrate where the thickness and density of the world
and my own emotional wounds
Throw up smoke screens
Obscuring its fierce and bright force

Open my eyes
Clear my vision
Make me aware of how my thoughts and words and
deeds
Affect the whole and those closest to me
Keep me vigilant in my self-awareness
That I may not get lost in distraction, stupidity
Or self-absorption to the degree that I cause harm in
the world
Ground me firmly in that meditative state where I can hear
the silence talking

Open my mind
That I may be curious and flexible in my thought patterns
Teachable and not calcifying as I grow older
But young and fresh and vibrant as I was in my youth
Ever ready for a new lesson a new understanding a new
way of being
Grant me the ability to communicate well and listen even better

Open my Spirit to receive You when You have work for me
as a Healer or a Poet or a Messenger or Teacher
Whatever you call me for
According to the current need
Teach me patience when I am not needed
when the times call for still reflection and non-action
in the fallow times when wisdom would have me wait

Teach me to attend to that which is core to living in harmony
With the will that co-creates reality each precious moment.

This is my prayer and my intent.

Break It Down

10-07-15

Another morning spent wrestling-
damn core issues are gonna be the death of me
In one corner is Love who is outside the box
Outside even the concept of the box
While on the other hand is the careful part of me
Who loves to remind me of every time I have been burned
Or wounded in love affairs
But her solution is to withdraw completely

I entertained the thought on my walk and
the tears flowed and the heart broke and here is my
answer for her

You are willing to live half a life
Because you think it is safe
I tell you no one gets out of here alive
Nothing is safe in the way which you desire

You are willing to walk away
From the big thrill
The true connection
The magic which has surprised me on all levels
Because you have no idea if anything more than what we
have right now
Will ever develop
I can only remind you that you do not know if the sun
will rise for you tomorrow
Though it will rise, you have no guarantee as to the
number of your days

If you could get this one thing we would be in cahoots:
Love is the only thing that does not change in this Universe
It may change its object, but allowed to fully blossom
it will grow and it will endure
There is nothing else worth living for
Whether it is in devotion to the Gods, to other human beings
to an ideal, to Music or Art,
to Nature
Love is the golden ring
I will not allow you to walk away from it because you
want a contract

At Full Gallop,
but Without Rider

10-12-15

The body makes its demands
and though it can build and hold a great deal of energy
the point comes when release is necessary
and must be taken
within the circumstances at hand

And so it was this past weekend
Upon more than one day
the demands were insatiable
and were satisfied as best as they could be
Yet physical satisfaction in and of itself
Has not been enough to fully sate me
For a long time

There are the satisfactions of a child
of an adolescent
and of a woman and Priestess
my hunger will not be quieted without multiple levels of
merging and meshing and
mutual satisfaction
in the here and now

This horse wants to be ridden
By an accomplished rider
Well in tune with nuances
when to trot and
when to canter,
when to build to a full gallop
and when to rest
until the urge to merge rises again

so I disbursed an excess of energy
several times
and even within that satisfaction there was frustration
Because I knew without a doubt
That my hunger for you encompassed more
Than a simple orgasm can provide

I quiver at the thought of a look
a touch
a kiss
hand holding
I am way gone this time
my desires are subtle and magnificent
Because you make my imagination catch fire
and my body is quick to follow
Satisfaction is a biological need
Desire for you encompasses all that I am
There is a world of difference between these two
and my bed will remain lonely until I can find you within it.

Contemplation of Zeus and Me

10-13-15

So today I was moved to wear your talisman
and as has happened before with very high energy pieces
There is some discomfort
Here I will try and understand from my tiny spot in the
Universe
Hoping when I have done so that you will give me input as well

I was drawn to the piece because its beauty
overwhelmed me
and I wanted it for me and for You
and Here it is

My encounters with you have been limited to the deep times
of Love and War for Dorothea
the most notable experience of You
was when you and Hermes drove out the alien wolf
appearing energy
at the full moon
with my hands planted on the altar and your then
talisman hanging in the light of the moon
As a marker of where I was
I remember the strike of your lighting
and curling up like a baby afterwards to recover
Because to use a funny expression that just came to mind
"it cleaned my clock"
It drove out everything and I felt empty
Safe but empty

So when I think of You
I think of vast energy
a Being who takes up the space of the skies
and is massively larger than I
There is little in my makeup of air
my comfort zones are fire and water and earth
and I have not tasted your energies that I can remember
other than that night

But I would be drawn to you if for no other reason
That I have altars to one daughter
and three of your sons
as if You saving my life were not enough motivation
Can You help me cross this bridge and let me know what
your take is on this?

the pathway for a child to her Father is Love
the heart is open naturally in that relationship
though you are mortal do you not know yourself for
one of my children?
Does the lightning not thrill you even when you watch
from your careful shelter
Have you not had intimate experience of its closeness
when in the higher elevations in Flagstaff?

Remember that My vastness can be a comfort to you
not something to fear
As you have imagined some days yourself a tiny pearl or
grain of sand in Hermes' hand
Can you not imagine me as a tender Being as well as fierce?
So many stories you hear, but if you listen carefully
In time I will tell you mine in a way that is perfect for you

Put up my image
hang the talisman there
I will let you know when to wear it

Give up your fear
that is no way to approach me

Woke Up in the Joy of It

10-17-15

Twenty years a Reiki Master
only twice has what happened last night occurred
both times this year
The first time was with a long standing friend
for the last twelve years, a teacher, someone I had done
ritual with
who had initiated me
had been in crises for awhile
Following guidance I had gone to his house after asking for
All his allies to help
After a long session
I felt myself as conduit for Reiki sink into core levels
Beneath all the struggle he had been going through
and that core to core bond was all that existed
For me the experience was absolute bliss
it aided him, shortly thereafter he was able to make the changes
He needed to do

Last night from my viewpoint was amazing
My practice with Reiki is just getting out of the way
I am a pane of glass
transparent and surrendered to that current
It operates as it will
the first session was normal
the second gave indications of being different
When I experienced the drunk state
at that point dizzy and not feeling well
I asked should I quit and got a resounding no
and in we went
to the core area
but with you the experience for me was bliss but absolute
core heat
So I sat and burned until the energy stopped

I woke periodically last night
at 6:30 finally gave up the fight for sleep
slightly foggy but absolutely joyous

I hope you are well

I am full of wonder at what the combination of the two
(thanks Janis)
brings to the table
Whatever shape we choose to give this magic between us
Let's not stop

Where Are My Wings?

10-19-15

I miss my lyrical Muse
my poems that float in the air or bob in the water
burn like fire or revel in earthly pleasures
These days my poems are like bricks
heavy and ponderous
exercises in extrication from emotional states
or exorcising emotional states
where is the fun, and the flow
where is my freedom dancing through the words
the laughter underscoring them
the joy as they fly out in their own dance?

I have grown too heavy with the coming of autumn
the harvests sweet and sour
somehow the season is oppressive
and I cannot locate the cause

my first reaction when spotting this trend was to run
As far and fast as I could from my existing life
which is not an impulse I have had for many years
only as a young wild horse of the zodiac
did I make that my M.O. until I one day realized the
futility of trying to run within
the framework of my being which took me to one end of
the country and then another
changing nothing substantial

So I stir my inner cauldron
I poke at the embers of the fire
I burn my fingers
wince and get better kindling than myself
I seek out comrades amongst the wild ones
human and otherwise
partners in crimes that harm no one
I take a very deep breath
and I feel her rise within me once again
as waves of warmth open me up to Her touch

Erato, I did call as my first Muse
and Her taste is as sweet as ever.

Who Drives the Big Rig?

10-20-15

So
thinking about us
You drive you
and I drive me
But as far as where we go
I think you should drive
You are more conservative and wiser
Me, I am crazy and a little reckless
I would have had us already meeting somewhere
between here and there
just to see how fast our motors would race

You are calm and peaceful
I am half the time trying to calm myself enough
That I can keep up with my emotions and passions
Without them riding over me
being around you brings this out more than usual
so if one of us is to have the lasso
and keep the runaway horse in line it would be you

You make me want to stir things up and shake things up
But that is because you rock me to my foundations
Sometimes that shakes stuff loose that I have to clean up
Most of the time it just delights the hell out of me
and I want more
But you have depths that calm me also
and I never ever want you to be pushed out of your
comfort zone
(seduced a little, charmed and persuaded a little, yes)
but only with your full and happy consent

So we are fine just as we are
Part of me knew that all along
I just had to have a garage sale and get rid of the parts
from the past
that are irrelevant to where we are and where we go
You have brought me into new territory within myself
I am in Aqua's arena now
and I am going to enjoy every second of it
this experience with you has rejuvenated me.

This is the Perfect Beauty

10-20-15

this is how things work in my life
and why joy is more often than not coming back to be
my constant companion.
as a direct result of giving healing through myself to you
a knot that had been difficult for me to cut loose
has been released
I hope your physical health has rebounded completely
because that was one heck of a gift

I do not know how we heal, whether receiving or
transmitting
Even with 20 years as a Reiki Master
I still call it magic
a gift
this time I had to clean house and write down the
characteristics of the illness
after having a healing crisis that knocked me for a loop.
but within hours of giving that part of me voice
the field was cleared and I felt and still feel 50 pounds
lighter psychically

I do not know how others clear things out
I have to write them nine times out of ten
and usually there are emotional charges attached which
sometimes feel
Like I am writing as I walk through a mine field
but when it is all clear, it is priceless
and whatever it took to get there is irrelevant at that point

So today, I took my walk
relieved some anger from the uncouth behavior of a co-worker
but then the joy just slid in next to me, took my hand
and we were off
The oaks in the upscale development are ancient
housing red-headed woodpeckers
crows
blue jays
quail
small sparrows
hummingbirds

the sun was shining in a gentle fashion
which is sometimes not the case in this valley called
Terra Linda
Sometimes the blaze is harsh and makes it difficult to
keep the clothes
that are suitable for work on the body
but on days like today, it is a gentle kiss and crown and
heart opener
next to writing - walking in nature - especially under the
good graces of nearby Mt. Tam
refreshes my heart and mind and spirit

Joy says remember my brother Gratitude
And I bow deeply in acknowledgment.

She Pokes Me, Erato

10-23-15

She is re-awakened within me
She is laughing in the background
" I never left; you just forgot to call on me
so the lyrical, erotic side of poetry did not flow easy
like it does when you take your delight with Me"

She poked me on my walk
as not just one but two dogs on separate occasions
came bounding up to me
When that happens I always feel like I am overshadowed
by Hekate
Who I make daily offerings to as well as the dark of
the moon
with Hermes
It always seems the dogs are looking through me and see Her
I only know that I laugh with joy to touch the dogs
and love them

She poked me when my mind turned to you, my love
Looking through time and space to find a place
where perhaps you still rested
as it is the wee hours of the morning when you finish
your work
and the fantasy that arose from that journey I will save
for another time
and another place more conducive to such explorations

My thoughts travel to you often
I struggle to discipline my mind in the morning at the
offering time
Meditation is clear of thoughts of you
But anything less than absolute focus will allow them
to come
and wind around my body
as if they were loving cats rubbing their scent upon my legs

Thinking of you always brings a powerful energy of love
heat,
desire opening the heart which brings joy
an expansion of Spirit and mind as well as I find myself
awaiting
the next time we meet

You Have a Way About You

10-24-15

Me, I talk a lot
It is my way, my tool, my calling card
my way to show what is inside
even the raw bits that would be hard to reveal
any other way

But you, when you say how you feel
You melt me utterly
Because you do so sparingly
and because when you do it you hit heart
or are a heat seeking missile
your accuracy and your timing are infallible
and you move me deeply

I am laughing right now from pure delight
because I love that you stimulate my heart and spirit
and mind
equally to the fire you can build within me
in a very short time
You take me on a journey where I enjoy who I am in a
new way
While just wanting to make love to you
In any way and every way I can

Right now I am both tired and stimulated as all get out
just writing those words gave me a rush from root to heart
warmth working its way up
Opening me up
Still and sweet and juicy
I want to touch you so badly I can hardly stand it
Which just is more kindling for my desire

May these words carry this sensation to you
You can wrap yourself in my heat and wetness
May it delight and please you as much as you do me.

Someday, beautiful man, I will touch you
and we both will tremble

We Return to Greet You

10-25-15

We come to you this time of year
When the veils are thin
and cold nights are clear
When you turn inside and are able to hear
We come to you this time of year

We come in love and we come in peace
We journey far so that we can meet
Share that which we know
With that which you seek
we all pursue the Mystery
From which we all feed

At least one time a year you know who we are
That all are related
that all share a bond
Whether you stand on our bones
Or we come after you
To be human is a constant
and we have all danced that tune

Watch carefully and learn
so much more you can see
this the final yearly harvest
will leave you a bill
for those things neglected
but also it will
Grant you the favors of work done so well
Just keep your hearts open
Your spirits will tell
As well as your Spirit
of steps needing to be taken
for the next year, please hear it

Draw courage in the strength
of those who passed before
Do not be too proud to ask for help
Whether you see them as ancestors
As watchers or guides
Do not waste this time
of the Samhein tides.

My Magnificent Distraction

10-25-15

I did not know I had this much passion inside me
Until you came along
Yes I had tasted it on an occasion here and
an occasion there
I have loved
not frequently
and not as well as I would have liked
I have bloomed late but baby,
Blooming I am
and it does not matter that it is at this point in my life
rather than that point
It only matters that it is happening
and if the passion does not bring me to my knees
The joy will
and moments of an excruciating tender flavor of love
Your happiness is my sweetest delight

My thoughts gravitate to you like
A navigator is drawn to the North Star
The flower follows the path of the sun
Seasons flow one after another
Each beginning and peaking and gracefully leading to the next
So my thoughts pursue you
Though we have not met face to face
I know the feel of you
the taste of your energy
the sound of your voice
You have shown me your heart from very early on
and your composure inspires me to embrace my own
still point

I can feel you when I write to you like this
It is as if you are listening
and you draw my words from me
like honey seeps from the fertile honeycomb
you draw sweetness from me that I did not know was
within me
because in my trust of you my walls have not tumbled
and fallen
but dissolved as if they never were
In my trust of you
I do not want walls, but want to let you come in as
deep as pleases you
There is nothing that I would hide from you
I want you to know me as I know myself
Light and dark
Fiercely strong and vulnerable
Capable of wisdom but still prone to storms of fire and water

I will never ever say again that this is not enough
This is more than I have ever experienced before with
one person
and I wake up grateful every single day with the thought
of you
First thing on my mind.

And when I am in my bed sliding into the quiet deep
where I take my comfort and strength and healing
You are the last thought before I go.

Two O'Clock in the Morning

10-28-15

So I go to sleep with a smile
Thinking about waking up
When you visit at closing time
Do you know that it is a thrill
Just knowing that you will come
There is an intimacy to tasting your energies
in the still of the night
as only a lover will do

I laugh at myself because
Since I cannot help reacting like a hormonal teenager
with you
I think I am just going to sit back and enjoy the ride
I want you
In any and all aspects you will open
and I am going to take my time savoring each and every
step we take
on this magical journey we have embarked on
Honestly, I have never been quite so excited physically
and emotionally
While deeply intrigued spiritually and intellectually as well
I think I had given up on that, thinking I was too hard
to please
No wonder I say I am undone

I feel like a woman caught in the pleasure of being
deeply and slowly seduced
as each time you find a new way to please me
Is like taking off another garment
Until I am standing naked before you
As I have so often said to you in the club
When you have woven music to enrapture and heat me
Please Don't Stop.

Last night when you played Buckets of Rain
once again you melted my heart
I think that you must know me well already
to hit the mark so exactly
I like it.

The Day's Treasures

10-31-15

To be open as a child is
To be fearless in the same way
To learn by listening and putting away these thoughts of self
that clamor all the time
a raucous noise that stills only in meditation
or moments of awe or connection powerful enough to
quiet it
The willingness to learn without preconception
The delight in another sharing their story
in a moment of abandon
a moment of risk that changes the game
and you know it even though you cannot see where the
new ripples lead

The deep gratitude that comes with Love
that watches it be ever new ever expansive
and makes you willing to meet its demands as long as
you are honored
by its Presence
The joy that you feel in just truly liking who someone is
Be it a friend or lover and remembering
That this is what makes life worth living
Letting it wash away the tiredness you sometimes feel
when life feels repetitive and stale and you wonder if you
have lost something
Precious that you used to carry
only to laugh because It still owns you and nothing
worthwhile has ever
been lost

Surprise
in a song
in a dance where the body finds a new groove
in that sense that something is unfolding around you
Within you
Within the whole of Creation
and if you can just capture the moment with all your
attention
It will reveal itself to you
It will change you
transform you into the awareness of the Gift
that has been within and without forever

Love wears so many faces
and never hides from you
It is you that have to remember
and step forth from the shadows where you have
become comfortable
take that gamble
take that tumble
Open your arms to that which awaits—share the bated breath

Letting Your Stream Seduce Me Early Sunday Evening

11-01-15

Lucky me
setting up the stream and the recorder for later
I have fallen into one of your hot hot hot themes
That and remembering this morning around 2:25am
Are having the effect that being in the club does
This heat between us has me vibrating on another level
and I like it

I am laughing right now because my mind is in a calm
sweet place
my heart carrying a quiet joy
but my body, oh my
There is nothing calm in my body
as song after song raises my temperature
gonna have to dance off some of this energy
because I am not at the point yet to release
But want to ride it a little more go a little higher
let it open me a little wider

When I was a youngster in my late teens
I never understood the rush to get from foreplay to
completion
as there was a world of thrills in building the energy
Young men do not appreciate that
and at the time I did not get their frustration
But then making love has always been about the journey to me
The intake of breath
the release of pheromones
the slow moan
the scent of sweat on skin

Learning each other's bodies and reactions
A world of discovery
Do it right and the coming together
Opens dimensions
Before the slide back into that sweet sweaty afterglow

Until it builds again and a new journey takes place

Right now I gotta dance.

Something Is Being Born

11-02-15

I started to feel it with the Samhein turning
a new energy
Grounding those things conceived this year
the new paradigm is fertilized in the womb of
Our collective consciousness
That balance is tipping
I now understand why months ago I just started
Clicking off the BS of the old one
There is no room in my head for that old story
of hate and stupidity and greed
There is no room in the coming world being born for that
Sorry doors closed

At the same time things are changing inside me
thought patterns are dissipating and shifting into a way
of being
Of course it was Love who sneaked in and set the fuse
for that explosion
She knows when I need to be tricked into some kind of
wisdom
She always has the easiest access
I see just today that people I have not heard the voices
of for a long time
Are all over my social media page
and they have some things to say
that I am happy to hear and share

It is no accident that this final harvest of the year
brought in its wash rain here and snow in the mountains
But today I caught a bit of understanding of my own harvest
I was feeling really good about my life
the people in it
Those I love immensely
Both friends and lovers
and then doubt stuck its nose in
and I simply said to it
Nope
I feel good because my reality is full of shining
beautiful compassionate beings
I acknowledge that I am one of them
and I am going to accept this as our birthright
and be happy
This is my reality
I claim it - I will fight for it - I will sacrifice for it -
I will offer myself utterly to the Love that delivers it
We all deserve it
It is the shape of our lives and how they should be and
how they will be

We are not here to be poor in Spirit
To have our children hunger and die
To feed some monstrosity of a corporate gloat
That is not our reality because we reject it with all of
our Being
And Mama and Pop gave us what we need to send the
vultures packing

So Mote It Be

Days as Gifts

11-03-15

There are periods
whether days or longer
sometimes an hour or a minute
Where the flow is spectacular
and the resulting opening within gratitude and love
Magnifies all the potential within each moment

Yesterday morning it rained
Only in a drought oppressed region
Can you know the enormity of what that means
Lifting you outside the normal framework that is now
lack of water
The smell of the rain drenched air
the moisture seeping into that that parched land
the cleanliness of it and the unmitigated delight and joy
it brings
are unparalleled

I took my walk in the afternoon
taking a gamble that the sunny part of the sky
Would not be overcome by the heavy black clouds on the
sidelines
There is a certain wind that blows hard and cold
You can feel it is a storm wind with rain once again in
its promise
I loved the feel of it on my skin
and walked just a little faster even though I was walking
against the wind
Exhilarated when I got back well run but dry

Driving home last night
the rainbow in the bay next to the bridge
just a fragmented frame of vivid color
The skies everywhere in the panorama
Were exquisite panels of gold and storm clouds
coral and light and dark playing
Wherever I looked whatever direction I took
revealed new beauty
and opened me up   bit by bit
to ecstasy and peace

The evening was lit by one who I love deeply
Still new enough to be thrilling
But those traits that complement and draw out the best of me
are becoming deeply endearing
and I plummet each day deeper into this Love
Reveling in being over my head
with someone I trust as a friend as well as a lover

I did not sleep enough but fell asleep easily and slept
like a baby.

Oh—Here It Comes Again

11-03-15

How is it possible that I have moved from being
tired and a little cranky
thinking that I have used up my stash of mojo
to having you on my mind and remembering how I feel
engaged with you
which now has me smoking and contemplating all sorts of
licentious acts

How is it that just the thought of you starts the same fire
I went to my bed with
Even though I am more fully satisfied each episode than
the prior ones
and the top of my head blows off and my sex explodes

How have you slid your sweet self under my skin
just your voice gets to me now
a line you type
on some level I hear you
and the effect your nighttime visits have upon me
is astounding
I would say my body is approaching a fever state
triggered by any and all contact between us

and I like it
and I want more
and I want to make you squirm and tremble and shake
like you do me
and I want to cross your mind every time you cross mine
I have become shamelessly greedy where you are concerned
Yet I would put your happiness and well being before
mine without hesitation

You intoxicate me
and it is this entire blend which makes it wholesome and
more powerful
than just a sexual obsession
had those and no thank you to any more
But with us it is this lovely mix of
Love and trust and mind-blowing chemistry

Desire Comes Creeping

11-05-15

Desire is licking around the edges
of my consciousness
I am standing here trying to work
and it keeps slipping in under the radar
It whispers your name
reminds me of how it feels when you are near
plays your voice in my ear
instead of on the stream or in a room of 50 people
it gives me the sweet imagination to hear you whisper
just to me
as it sends shivers up and down my backbone

I am starting to get warm now
The room is cool
and I stand near a window
But this heat comes from inside
from the deepest root it runs up my legs
and focuses on the core between them
Desire has no respect for boundaries or where I am or
what I am
Doing my very best to focus on
it whispers your name again
Remember it says
Remember how it feels when you have been dancing and
chatting
and you are wet and hot and touching yourself till you
scream his name again

How can I possibly forget?

At the point of 24 hours without visual or chat
Even though I know you will sweetly visit
and wake me when you do
The craving begins
I can try to ignore its presence but that just makes it
more stubborn

It knows where I want to be
Cares not a hoot if I get sleep
There will be no satisfaction until there is some degree
of a deeper union once again
(If it had its way with me and all things were possible
I would be in your bed right now)

Some days it is only believing this may someday be
possible that makes the physical distance between us
Bearable at all.

Woman on Fire

11-05-15

Praying that she has not lost the thread
That came at the beginning of her walk
Dedicated to Pan and Brigid
and which she had asked for a hold placed upon it
By them
Until she was able to write

Woman on fire,
as a younger woman she thought she had no passion
Unless it were lit by sex on rare occasions
or music which always had stirred her soul
As she walked she felt herself young in this way
She felt young in being herself, which had taken so very
very long

She saw herself as a creature of fire
But her feet firmly grounded and part of the earth she
strode upon
as this was not a fire that consumed her and left the ash
of the Phoenix bird
This was a fire that she burned within
Lived within
and carried the charge of to those she loved

This was a fire twinned in the man
Who had the incontestable claim to her heart
Her joy her delight and her long awaited friend and lover
the one who knew her in an instant
and she him
Though the unwinding between them happened in
delicious layers
as one savors an exquisite meal slowly
no hurry no rush no goal no end in sight

This was a fire that rose in mystic dreams
In contact with the Gods and Goddess
Whose service was her life blood
her purpose
her reason for still being incarnate
though again her thoughts are drawn to the Priest
who she knows has lessons for her
and she for him

As she burns she stands outside herself
and sees herself transparent
with the afternoon sun shining through her
as if she were a prism
and many colors fractured through her
as if she is giving birth to a rainbow

As she returns to the part she plays at work
She is struck by an overwhelming gratitude
For being who she is and alive and in love with so much
in her world
This is the best of her life to date
65 approaching 66 years and full of an incandescent joy

Thunderstorm

11-07-15

Sometimes bursting into tears is the storm that comes
when conditions have built tension
That can only be relieved by its exploding into release
That was what the tears did this morning
A combination of stress, poor diet and not enough sleep
Along with the Universe evidently not lining things up
exactly the way
I wanted them last night
(Laughing)
triggered an explosion of cleansing water
to relieve the emotional blocks

The path appears to be clear
I can live in such a way that I follow as it is marked out
Step by step
Whose hand holds the marker?
Our hand does
I sat in the car for a moment last night and thanked
every living being
For sharing this journey with me, for being my teacher.

All I really know is that there is Desire and there is Love
There is Will
and these are all good
Then there is the lust for results
and that can feel like sticking an ice pick in one's own heart

Kind of like it did this morning

I slowly am learning that these powerful feelings
Change like the weather patterns
Except for Love which will grow consistently if I get
out of the way
And don't lay my plans on it
Because like a wild stallion it will throw that shit off
its back
I can own my feelings
and learn through the interplay of shadow and light
and all is well
But when I start to project them onto any given
situation with others
I am poisoning the waters we swim in

Love talked to me this morning as I wept
and reminded me that She is never the One thwarted
Desire chuckled and reminded me that She is always good
then Insecurity sheepishly stepped forward and said
"Yep, it was me again. Sorry for messing up the party.
You know I always want everything in writing, as if Life
were some paint by numbers picture."

If it were like that it would kill me instead of being this beautiful
Powerful chaotic rush that is filling me with energy and delight
This very moment

I thanked Insecurity for being honest
My tears dried
and I was grateful for everything once again
As if a child with absolute trust
Who approaches it all as an unfolding adventure.

Just Say Yes

11-09-15

Tonight the heart had to break open some more
It starts with a constriction
I have no choice but to zone in on that center
and go deep deep deep to get past the armoring
not for the feeble minded or weak of Spirit
This job I signed on for called incarnating
But I am all the way in

So after it began to crack open
I followed its pure impulses
and I got out of bed
and let it lead me
bread crumbs were glowing in the dark
and these words dancing in my head
As I first petitioned and then made my promises
Because all the road signs only pointed in one direction

Just Say Yes
just say yes to knowing your own heart
dancing in your own center
Giving it all up and letting the chips fall where they may

Just say yes to opening when you can
to surrendering when you cannot
to letting it flow over you through you and around you
as it will
The only obstructions are the old house of cards
The way you used to live when you did not know any better
But now you do

Sometimes all you can do is just say yes
When it all feels wrong
When you feel lost and helpless and clueless
when the street signs all point in different directions
go deeper go through any pain any blockage
or if you cannot just sit at the crossroads

Wait
Because that Love train is gonna come through
maybe now
maybe in the next flow of time picking at your innards
But it will come

Now I can sleep again.

Ah
Evidently we are not through
More is coming through
Take care darling child
Take care that in your melding and merging and loving others
That you do not lose yourself nor place your dreams as
a burden
Upon another soul in its freedom
Let there be a sacred space between you where you may meet
When in accord to do so

Give that free flying beautiful Spirit walking next to you
All the acknowledgment that you can
when you see it manifesting its gifts and its sorrows
Know it in Love
If you are fortunate enough to walk together in time
for a little bit
Savor it
enjoy it utterly and completely
Learn from each other
Dance out your joy and your heat
But always be ready to let go
If freedom calls your paths to diverge
and know their heart as you would know your own
Love never disappears

Trembling

11-11-15

your voice in my head
the sweet warmth of your energy
has raised goosebumps on my skin
and butterflies in my gut
I breathe deeply on purpose as I watch myself vibrate
in response
to the degree of contact we share
I revel in it
like swimming naked in a hot springs
You have gotten to me
I have gotten to you
and oh how very delicious it is

The palms of my hands are open chakras
everything tingles and is sensitive to the currents
words are the way I play when you are not here
the way I want to tease and please and tantalize you
as you do me
they carry my smile and my laughter and my sheer delight

and for now they have stopped and my weary head seeks
the pillow.

Surrounded by Fire

11-12-15

I smolder
Not yet at a burn
the heat alternates between a cocoon of warmth
with sparks at the heart of it
to a rising flame that consumes as it pleases
and I the voluntary kindling

All it takes is a thought of you
your voice in my head
the amount of heat that oh so well designed and
embodied image
I connect with you
conveys
I will admit I use the zoom function in moderation
As it is just too much
like standing too close to a raging bonfire
or the blazing summer sun when your skin says look out

So there is heat
and there is passion
and there is desire
and there is lust
and I live within the co-mingling of these similarly
flavored
but finely nuanced states
for much of my day
the best times catch me completely off guard
during the workday
and I bask in the joys of my body and heart
just contemplating the man that you are

Sometimes, like last night
A boy will approach me in the club
and I don't even know what to say to them
Usually it is a gentle way of saying
Hey I am dancing with my friends
That is why I come here
Even were I to say
it takes time for a boy to grow to be a man
Goddess knows that it has taken me decades to find you
and no one else ever came close to matching me as well
as you do.

Fever Just Keeps on Rising

11-14-15

Being close to you
Watching you move
No - actually that is not when it started tonight
It started before I came into the club
You popped up and said something
My nipples got hard
I became flushed
and soft and wet
and forgot whatever it was that I was doing

If I keep it building
Gonna end up being hot all the time
and distracted
with you riding my mind
The way I want to ride your body
Slow and lazy until I cannot stand that pace anymore
and let you flip me over and pick the pace we move at

I want to taste every inch of you
investigate with my eyes then my tongue and mouth
then my hands
Knowing I will never get my fill
I pray to the heavens above
that I get the chance to try
and if not, I am gonna just ride this good kind of crazy wherever
It takes me
It will not do me in -but no doubt it will change me
all for the better

It's a funny thing
If you were not who you are
With your sweet soul and kind heart
I would not have this passion rising to critical mass
because it takes the whole package to move me this much
I don't play for anything less
right now I cannot write because I am on fire

Holding Space

11-15-15

I have not wanted to leave the temple I call home
since Friday night
I did yesterday and the world feels like pain and grief and sorrow
There is nowhere to go except as deep as possible
There is nothing to do but witness
Listen and share
However I am led to
and right now other than the need to write this morning
I just want to seek and rest in the stillness

We have all known the structures are being shredded
and they should be
as there are too many negatives in the world we have
collectively created
Sometimes there is no easy way to break it down
so that what is left is that which is of lasting value
I am being told right now focus on that which I crave
From the depths of my being bring it forth
As the shielding for
When I walk out of the door and view the world

Justice
Peace
Love
Respect for all living
Unity
Healing
Compassion
Empathy

No doubt you can add to this list
My heart says as the tears run down my face
That if I focus on the negatives that are all coming to
the surface

because they must be acknowledged and transformed
I can get caught into thinking they are the only reality
and I will not be able to survive that way
nor even move from this spot

I have a friend who knows how to take me deep
Without me saying I need that shelter
His gift is music and total immersion within it
In fact I would say that every friend I have
In physical form and not
Is telling me that now
Go to the heart of the matter
risk it all for Love and do not think that in your small arena
You cannot have an effect
It is only in your own life
That you can effect change
Small steps daily
Sometimes only being able to deal with the present moment

When everything around you is in chaos and feels like it
is moving
like a freight train at 90 miles going off the tracks
Slow yourself down
Find the antidote within yourself
Then bring it up
Bring it out
Share it
Focus on it
Give your life for it

It hurts like a bitch right now
I am told to close with these words

We Got This
We signed on for it
We have had our warrior's hearts shaped and primed for it
We have Big Backup

The Gift of You

11-15-15

I woke up about 8 am
checked in with myself
and realized I was in shape to get up
Surprisingly enough
The smile I wore on my face when I slid into sleep
with the aid of an Amethyst crystal and some Reiki
To balance and calm the state of high energy
that our dance had engendered
Was still on my face when I woke up
My thoughts and heart full of you

You are such a gift to me
The last two nights under the spell you weave
So adroitly
Have charged me when the world is drowning in sorrow
Brought me joy
and heat
and the freedom to experiment with the velocity
Of sexual energies allowed to play as they will
without a need to (note there was desire to)
Decide if they should be released in one kind of ecstasy
Or ridden and allowed to express as they will in new ways
Bliss in and of itself to be able to share that experience
with you
Wisest thing I did all this year was to listen to Aqua
and come back into the club
and just love you without strings or fear

My body awoke with this undercurrent
a hum of energy
fully charged
light and vibrant
open in the heart and everywhere else
and it feels like this new amalgam being created
out of equal parts Love, Desire, Healing and Joy is
Today, or at least this morning, to be offered
In the service of the Muse who rides me

I cannot even find the words to tell you how I feel
about you
and I hear a soft whisper in my ear
He knows
May the Holy Powers give me time to show you
in whatever ways we both deem appropriate
However and wherever it is possible
For as long as it is a joy and revelation to both of us

I ain't going nowhere

Dammit, I Would Rather Write Love Songs

11-16-15

I want a short cut
I want a quick fix
I want to learn from the pain of mistakes instantly
and to the degree where I never repeat them
I want this for all of us

I want to write love songs
I want to feel the power of Love that is so immense
That it swallows everything that is not it
Love that is a steam roller and rolls all over everything
that is not it
and mashes it into the ground
where it just becomes fertilizer for healthy things to grow

I want a miracle
I want us to wake up and look at the blood on our hands
and say we have had enough
that we can see this never ever solves anything
and wake the fuck up and stop this endless cycle of
destruction and killing

I want to understand the Goddesses Who Embody both
Love and War
I want Them to tell me how Destruction is as Sacred
as Love
Because I am feeling so very human these days
and so very sad and tired of this current cycle
I don't know how to carry what I see
Within my heart or my head or my spirit
I don't know how to function in a healthy way
Within the day to day

I want to write love songs
I want to celebrate all that is whole and vibrant and
good about humanity
I want to see our common bonds, our common desires,
and our healthy impulses
At the very least I want to see a balance
Because I do not want to add all this shit
To my own inclination to annual depression this part of
the year
Because I will drown under the weight of it

I want to find my heart-song, my song of joy and rebirth
and I want that to flow instead of blood, and hate and
recrimination
I have had enough
Haven't we all?

Surely we are ready to collectively come up with
something better.

Cannot Get Enough of You

11-21-15

It is not just the heat
The spark that triggers a slow burning fire
ain't never gonna go out

It is not just the groove
when we move together
Cause the rhythm of that ain't never gonna fade

It ain't that you know me
and know how to please me
Or that dancing to your tune
Rocks me body and soul

It ain't the jewel of your heart
That opens and provokes mine

It ain't that x-factor, factor of cool to the natural hip
the jazzy smooth vibes that make me wanna flip
the sultry slow motions that the ocean recall

Oh baby sweet baby it is the sum of them all

It is that unknown unknowable connection
that just is
It follows both daytime and nighttime
Where it is
Woven in my dreams
A smile upon waking
as if you left a taste
of where you have touched me

I won't ever get enough

It Got Real Simple Tonight

11-26-15

I sit here and it is more than time for me to seek the comfort of my bed
Yet I am still full of what you make me feel every time I see you
this delicious combination of respect and love and heat
I like who you are and I have from the first time that I talked with you
It makes me happy to be around you
Fuck the circumstances
They are not perfect
But we live within circumstances our entire lives
and to have such a clean clear feeling is a godsend

As long as you are happy to see me walk in the room
I am gonna be there

As long as I can do anything to support you to bring you joy
to tease and make you laugh
I am gonna be there

You bring out the best in me
and more than that you bring out me
Because you have this complete non-judgmental acceptance
That heals
That brings me more open and more willing to be seen
Than almost anyone else in my entire life
and I wonder if you know what a gift that is

Like a moth to the flame baby
I cannot help but be moved by you
and drawn to you
and thinking of my words tonight I realized
If this is the longest case of foreplay in the world
If touching you energetically is as far as we go
I am all the way in it
Because there is more juice to this
Than I have had with most people I have loved
and it is a treasure just exactly as it is

I accept that I am always gonna want a life partner
whether monogamous or polyamorous or whatever the
hell manifests
I have wanted that kind of bond my whole life
and if I do not get it I am still gonna love with every
fiber of my being
and I will live without regret because I am putting it all
on the line
From here on

I hope I am around you for a long time no matter what
the circumstances

Pruning the Branches

11-26-15

Woke up this morning crying
Because my fantasies are not reality
Seems some part of me is still a child
Who thinks Disneyland is real
and that everything should come wrapped up in the
perfect wrapping
With the perfect gift inside
Trouble is that this very attitude or childish need
Is what keeps blinding me to the fact that
Everything I need and want is already here
Blinders off sunglasses on vision improved

I have scripts about birthdays from childhood
that punishment and reward system for good behavior
Rather than using love to raise and guide kids
Damn, how the hell did we get stuck in that model?
I am happy to see that looking around at the families I know
There seems to be a lot less of that
Anyhow
Birthdays mess up my head
I want everybody to say Happy Birthday
Then I want the focus to be on something or somebody else
Sometimes I just get tired of living in this emotional
smorgasboard
I call myself
No wonder meditation is such a joy
When I am calm enough to do it
at least the chatter stops for a bit

Here is what I know in truth:
I am loved and I love
I am learning and growing – I ain't dead yet
I am healthy and blessed with the gift of Reiki and healing
I have tools I forget to use that help when I do
remember
I really do not give a damn that my fantasies may never
ever pan out
As long as it stays as interesting as it is now
As long as I am viable in giving back in some way
As Priestess
As Lover
As Divine Human in these times of intensity
Thank goodness for the Gods and Tribe
Together we will make it through
Together we will make it better

I don't mind a little bleeding or a few tears along the way
Cleans up and marks passages for me

The Gift

11-26-15

The first group meditation
once the breathing captured me into stillness
the God came
and in that communication that is beyond words
He showed me the error of my ways
He showed me His love His energy
In each of the men that I love

" Foolish child, why do you insist that I come to you in
any one
Particular form
When instead you could be within the bliss of loving Me
In each of these and more
I give you a waterfall and you bring out logs to make dams"

At this point we laughed together

The second part of the group meditation
Was a kundalini progression
From root to crown
That was such good medicine I still tingle from it
As if my insides just came from a hot tub or hot spring
but revitalized as well as relaxed

At the third chakra voice went out
We had just started to progress with chant on our own
at the heart chakra
When voice came back on
The suddenness of the sound returning
Opened me and brought happy tears

I think I am going to take this next solar year
and practice being very kind to myself
Betcha the rest of the world will really appreciate that
cause there is no such thing as doing something to myself
and not doing the same to All

I cannot even begin to express my gratitude for this lifetime
and everything I have been given

Captured

12-06-15

Aware of you all day but especially this afternoon
As if you had left your scent on my skin
The flavor of you upon my tongue
Your voice in my head your whisper tickling my ear
The way a song long remembered brings back everything
that happened when the imprint was left

Peak experiences leave their mark
I have had many at your hands
but nothing like last night
and doors of perception that open never really close again
A warning given me decades ago; still
I will approach with curiosity and fearlessness
When a new one beckons

you are such a door
the further in I come the deeper I want to come
the more I know of you the more I want to know
There are moments when I feel that I have touched
you physically
but to dwell on that is to torture myself with longing
and I would so much rather take delight in what is
As it is
here and now

If you have left Desire as a mark within me
at the same time you have left peace and satisfaction
Delight and fulfillment
Growth
and Happiness

I welcome your visits
something is being built between us
Come what may it will do us well
Life is too short and I have had too many years
without the delight of a friend and lover your equal
You satisfy my adventurous spirit as well
Like any good magic man
I never know what you will pull out of the hat next
nor what wonders you will manifest

This thing between us is a thing of great beauty
and the mystery dances within it
Laughing its ass off
Fun

Never Far Away

12-08-15

Just a thought away
A feeling that arises
Does it originate from you or from me?
I do not know because the moment I am conscious of it
I feel you near
Especially if it is in the times I would expect you to be awake
Sometimes I feel as if you wake up first
and then the thought of you, the desire or the love
or all of the above awakens within me at the same time

It changes
How I respond to this beauty between us
There are times when I am hot with need for you
But there are also times more recently when the
thought of you is like basking
naked in the rays of a hot golden sun
content and stretching out like a lithe cat
feeling myself from head to toes
In a luxury of well being
Because you are here in this world
and you have allowed me in

Each time we come together something new is woven
into the fabric
a stronger thread of connection
I feel as if a weight has been lifted
I have been watching for you
for about a decade
because I had a reading then where I felt you and was
told in time you would appear
In my life
I had nearly forgotten it because time is such a tyrant
I had thought it only the deepest dream my heart carried
and had accepted that reality had shifted you out of my
field of potentiality

Second Life has been such an enormous gift to me
many things that could not manifest anywhere else
have arisen there
Many joys and new aspects of myself have been born
and I am happier than I have ever been
You, my darling one, are at the top of the list of joys
and I am so very very grateful

Aphrodite indeed rules in-world for me
May it ever be so
May I ever serve her well
She is whispering in my ear that you are a favorite son
Did you know that?

Child of the Day,
Woman of the Night

12-10-15

Since I am living with this split now for a year
With it just intensifying as I am more and more drawn
to you
and the night hours
contemplation of it has sprung up
including acknowledging that when I started my focus
on Hecate
with the dark of the moon ritual for Her and Hermes monthly
several years ago
There was an affinity and love for the depths of the
night begun
This did make the dark half of the year commutes much
much easier

In these times, daytime is for work
the breaks within what is at worst doing time
and at best Priestess work in the environment I find
myself in
Are the lovely Marin walks for half an hour
and lunch in the cafe downstairs where I can disengage
for a bit and eat good cheap food
Even the weekend days now are for sleeping in after
pushing the boundaries of time and energy
Because I love you and the nights
Something tries to tell me that you cannot spend your
nights dancing and loving
I say - where is that written?
I am not making that the whole of my life
my hunger for it is in balance and response to a kind of
bondage to my days
and the system I am subject to until the path clears
for retirement

My desire for it will never wane, it is within my deepest nature

My spirit comes alive in other ways as well
The poetry, especially the highly inspired ones written in
tandem with Higher Self driving
or Deity communications are as necessary to me as
breathing
Reiki has absorbed my life in the 22 years I have
practiced it
and it is my joy to be used by it as a conduit
I cannot imagine being alive without it

Perhaps this is also a good thing – this limitation
Because the pull you have on me is so powerful
Laying on the table last night receiving my healing
I allowed myself to go into the depths of my heart and found
you have taken up residence there – moved in quite
comfortably
I have welcomed you in and only want to go further and
deeper into loving you
Yet given our circumstances I cannot let that consume me
as if we were building a life together
Something is being built, and I know it
but it is stone by stone
slowly and carefully
and whose hand orchestrates it besides us I do not know
What I do know is that body and mind and spirit are
aligned with my heart
where you are concerned

Which is why when you expressed your pleasure with
the poem recounting
the full bonding between Loki and I under the
necessities of war
You were the final catalyst to what had been building all day
and energetically I was charged and simultaneously
deeply in love with Him
and you
I do not wonder that I could not sleep
I am amazed that I ever did go to sleep
Something about laying down on the couch with your
voice in my ear
and the undercurrents of the music
brought me quiet peace in tandem with the ecstatic heat
I was riding

May you feel and know the joy that was upon me
When you said you would lie down next to me soon

Love is holding me so firmly this day
I snuggle into its embrace as a child to her Mother.

Here I Am

12-12-15

In much the same state as I was before
Sleep captured me in a sweet drift
as the snow will lay a layer upon the landscape overnight
I burn
I yearn
In meditation both my heart and lower chakra wide open
Yes
this was how I was when you left
Burning with heat and love and a desire to touch physically
So overwhelming that I spoke to the Lady of it
She laughs because She knows my predicament and has Her hand
firmly within it

Last night or should I say this morning in the quiet hours
the wanting to touch you was so strong I thought
it would draw me to you
that I would find wings and be in your locale
the desire to lay naked spooning with you
gave me an almost visual with the sensation of how good
that would feel
until the intensity was such that I sought a quiet place
that I asked Her to create for me to shelter
Where I might burn
If I am not burning with you as the flames increase and
the glow captures me
Then I will burn here alone

Although I must admit this concept of alone is not
working right now
As I feel our connection
and even as I was sequestered and consumed this morning
there came a point where the Siamese twins of Love and Desire
Simply consumed me and filled me within a state
That did not find itself wanting in any way
I simply was
I was the Desire
I was the Heat
I was the Yearning for touch in the physical realm
I was happy and at peace
Because I was completely at home in that state
Recognizing it as my true nature

You should know that you have me now
Wide open
Loving you wanting you
Desiring your happiness as much as my own
Darling this is a wondrous state you have left me in
If it pleases you I can only hope you feel the same
As there is a complete, rare and precious joy within it.

Beauty of the Connection

12-14-15

There are periods of grace or darshan or whatever word
expresses the flavor
they are not always evident before or during
because there are many pieces in how we relate to each other
Why we seek guidance or help
and only the Gods know why magic can be transmitted
within objects
charged in order to connect more firmly with the Gods
Last night was a night of superb beauty
that started out with me being exhausted and feeling
quite off kilter

I had just about given up on the night and my low energy
But had forgotten I wanted to record the Jazz night set
So I logged back on with the intent to just go to bed
and give my body what it most wanted
Instead I found the set was live an hour early and
could not resist going
But I was still drained and semi burned out
I could not bear the state I was in since I have been
missing this set
and mourning it all of this year

So I contemplated for a moment
and since it was that low-energy
Where is the Love? pitfall that hurts the most
I sought Aphrodite
I asked permission to wear the talisman
drenched myself in the rose oil
and watched myself change in harmony with Her
who I serve more and more these days
I had a wonderful time for awhile
and then as I felt the gradual slide down in energy
Found my heart totally immersed in love for you
and our words entwined to a degree that took my breath away

Again I was ready for bed
But this time with a smile in my heart and on my face

Here is where the Mystery stepped into the scene
I was talking to a friend who had been struggling a
couple of days
and was in pain
and it was not until we were done with a pretty deep
conversation
For half an hour
That it was very clear to me that I did not know if any
of the communication was from me
and if so it was minimal compared to the
strength and power of the communication from the Lady
through me
and I was humbled once again
that I could serve as a vehicle when Her presence is
most needed

For this alone I would be on the planet
Yet I have been given so much more
Writing these words I feel my heart as if it is
swallowing me up
and I burn within this Love with a soft golden glow
a Heat that melts obstacles to being Love within my life
Wherever I am, whatever I do

There is nothing that I ask for more than just this.

Aberration

12-17-15

What causes the aberration of forgetting how much
Love there is here?
Reeling today because I had let slip my anxiety at work
to another executive
Who has spent the day checking on me to be sure that
I know
That there is nothing critical to worry about
This is a man that I do not have a lot of contact with
But I have always striven to be kind and considerate of
him in our encounters
and that has come back to me today

There is mindfulness that is aware of the big picture
and I go for months and months with that holding
pretty secure
Within my day to day life
What is it that weakens that understanding?
Is it duress or is it just a crack in my own
consciousness and understanding
That allows that negativity to take hold
It takes no effort at all for me to look at the 65 years
of life
and see the hand of Love and Grace that has led me
through this lifetime
From being born too early and spending the first month in
a hospital room
Until yesterday's firm guidance through unusual and
trying circumstances in the morning
Ending in a lovely healing in the evening
I have never ever been without the aid and loving that I needed
Though granted I have had my share of bleak times that
blinded me to the reality
Again it is that tunnel vision that cannot see the overall
pattern

I suppose this is part of us growing up
Not just me
But humans
For critters who think we are so smart
We are a little slow
But evolve we must and evolve we will and are
I am fixing to remember upon demand
Keys on a rainy sidewalk
or a hundred other examples of how tight I am held
It is my responsibility to cultivate a mindset that
embraces and holds this fast
The fluidity of who I am demands a keen eye
an observant attitude
and a calm and present Heart

When I am where I want to be then the real fun begins
I get to play with others of like mind
and joy spills over my fingers like a waterfall
or love grows so large as to leave me shaking and
trembling from its magnitude.

Down, Girl, Down

12-18-15

So the thought of you came floating through the air-ways
My body stood up with a bullseye in her middle
and that magic combination occurred
thought - body - desire
and all I am hearing while I struggle to concentrate on work
Is Friday night!
Friday night!
I have told her to store up the energy and I am with
her 100%
I want to see you with all of myself attending
Flesh - heart - spirit - mind
I miss you more as time goes on

I found myself imagining you last night
With your reading glasses on
Reading the poems
and it was so delicious to me to know
That what I write and post gives pleasure to you
in many ways it is the most intimate thing I can share
with you
Especially long distance
and your delight frees little knots within me that I
didn't even know I had

I was reading yesterday about how precious it is for us
to give each other
Full attention
Full and complete acceptance without judgment
This is a gift you have given me from day one
and I am mindful of it with others and how I approach them
Because it is as if we give each other the very best
environment to thrive
When we do this
Allowing ourselves to drop filters and to be real
Is like taking a breath of pure oxygen after nearly
suffocating
Way too rare in the madness of the culture at large

So my body can and will smolder at the thought of you
Me, the rest of me, the all of me
Has a deeper hunger for your presence
Your voice in my head
your warmth and your totality
I breathe deeper around you

Loving Ain't Hard

12-20-15

Loving ain't hard
Being human sometimes is
The limitations we carry within us
are not measured by how well we do anything
Except access our own happiness and with that the
happiness
that we transmit and give freely to others

The discontent that comes upon me
Is easy to put upon anything in the world
Except where it belongs
Whatever my reaction is to what is
which tells me anything is not good enough
Anything that tells me life is flawed
Is a lie
Life contains all things
Joy, sorrow, death, rejuvenation, ecstasy, boredom
Life is change
If I seek the changeless
There is only Love that does not change
How we act in the name of love
how we treat each other
How we fail love
none of these can diminish what it is
and that never changes

Everything else does
I sit here and my devotion for and to you
Is overwhelming
and that is never the source of misery
The source of my own misery is when I have some
fucking idea
As to what I should be receiving
You owe me not an iota of anything
My love is free and easy and binds not
Desire

Well desire can be problematic
But it is not your job to satisfy that either
Your only job is to be the best man you can be
As mine is to be the best woman

(None of my deal breakers have been triggered
You have always been honest and truthful
You have always been kind
You have given me the gracious feeling of being
Safe and protected when you are around)
(Not sure how you do that)

What we give to each other must be done freely
Without expectation
Without regret
Without the burden of need
With respect and mutual acknowledgment
That not being perfect lovers
Does not mean that Love is anything less

It just means we are human
Me, where you are concerned
I am in it for as long as you want me around
and as long as I am capable of putting Love first

If I have wants and needs beyond what we are able to
give each other
Then it is on me to satisfy them elsewhere
I will not make them a burden around your neck

From the beginning I promised you unconditional Love
and I will hold myself to that standard
Because I promised it and because you deserve nothing
less
My fine, beautiful, good and loving man.

Winter
After Yule
2015

Dreams or Madness

12-22-15

He said to me last night that I feel too much
and that such a path carries hurt

You said something about dreams coming true

I stand here looking at the glorious sky filled with blue
and gray and black
from the marriage of rain clouds and the newborn sun
and I ask
How can I feel less?

I like to burn with the intensity of my heart
at its most honest
Because I feel life then
I feel Love
I feel passion
and within those states at their most intense
I feel the Spirit that all arises from
I feel the Timeless kiss we mortals
who are bound too much to that which is less than we
are designed for
hardly ever see.

I feel and I burn and I dream these dreams that I
cannot share
except with my closest friends who know and love me
even if my dreams are madness
I imagine realities where I am more free and living a
simpler life
Where I am mated and happy and building a life with a
lover who is easy to love with no drama
Where I am free to teach and write and wander land that
I love
Where I can find community of like minded ones
and in our own way do our parts towards making a better world

I will not see these dreams bear fruit in all the ways I wish
But the children will

When I leave here I will be given different work
In a different form
with maybe different Allies and maybe not
But I will be damned if I want to leave with any regrets
for not loving enough
or living enough or giving enough or feeling and dreaming
enough

I want to cross over regretting nothing and grateful for
every moment here

If that is feeling too much then I say let me feel more
and let me give the joy of it to a world that feels too little.

The Song I Continue To Hear

12-24-15

It is a melody my spirit hears but not my ears
it underscores every day with joy
with gratitude
Patience and compassion
As I let the lessons of this year settle into my bones

The bumpy parts were the catalysts for the gifts grown inside
like the pearls that spring from great irritation
the tough lessons teach me about endurance and love
Strength within and the great Love that sustains me
Even when I feel bleak and overwrought
The gifts that appear out of nowhere
From Deity or people
the connections that strum through the web
that make me vibrate as the tuning fork I know myself
to be
That enable me to focus on another and when I am very lucky
Place me in situations where I can easily make their
journey a little easier
Being the right place at the right time for them is a
tremendous gift

What can I say about this year?
Reiki has come out stronger and truer and blown up
more ideas
of obstacles that do not exist for it
and expanded my ability as conduit
Which to this day I believe was the prequel to both my writing
and my aspecting work
as I had been trained to step back and let Source energy
use me as it will
knowing that this is bliss this is Love this is service and
this is joy

The people, oh my, the people who entered my life
the strengthening of existing ties that bind
the love the delight the surprise the mystery
Oh yes, in my still heart there is a great big shiny ball of
Love and Peace
from these encounters and my world expanding

Spirit giggles in the background and whispers
You have no idea, I have barely begun

The lovers, when did I get to use that word in plural?
Three have stolen my heart
Though the primary shifted mid-year unexpectedly
Each is a jewel in my life
Each teaches me about Love
Wisdom
and walking my talk
Each is a friend as well as a lover

I count every gift of this year today
Even those periods of oppressive demands at work
Which sapped my energy and asked for more
Breaking me down and making room for the new to enter

I have written more than in any other year
I have gone deeper in order to do so
I have let go of old crap
I have welcomed new shit
I really need to improve my vocabulary

Praise to the Gods and Goddesses who love me!
Praise to the artists, the Priests and Priestesses, the
Spirit Workers!
Praise to the men who love themselves and women!
Praise to the teachers, the musicians, the hermits, the
peacemakers!
Praise to the activists who do so by stealth!
Praise to the lovers, the sisters, the brothers!

Praise to those still who come out but rarely, bringing
us meaning when we may be
flailing!

Praise to the Makers, the Shapers, Those who wait in
the wings!
Praise to the Dreamers, all who make our spirits Sing!
Praise to those who said Yes to Great Sacrifice
To awaken the rest to humanity's plight!

Praise to all Created and Uncreated!
Praise to the Emptiness!
Praise to the Stillness!

Praise to Those who bring the Rain to a world with
such thirst!

Thank You

New Territory

12-25-15

My body hums it sings it whispers
It remembers
Still in the state of desire
Satisfied in the wee hours but not sated
I see how it is between us
Hot and fluid and primed for action
Were you here or I there I would be ready and willing
and happy
Just to wash myself up and have another go

I had no choice but to bring myself over that edge last night
Feeling you at the same time was unbelievable
and has left me aware that I will continue to just want
you more
Wanting feels good feels like life and healing and
expansion
Feels like home
Feels like a missing piece fitting back into my psyche
as if not wanting you was the aberration

You are a joyous adventure

I am your play-land your safe harbor your comfort zone
You are my favorite bringer of bliss
My well-spring of desire
my perpetual source of heat and flame
the match to my gasoline
Or the gasoline to my match
Either way we are combustion

and we are peace
and friendship
and companionship and love

I have gone over the edge and I ain't coming back
I will enjoy you however and wherever and whenever I can
and look forward to the next time
As I writhe and burn but do not touch when away from you
Why would I want an appetizer alone
When, with the patience to wait
and live within the burning
I can share the whole meal with you.

Darling One.

The Currents Flow

12-27-15

My body is loose this morning, relaxed
Still sopping wet from the morning's union
and my prolonged finish which left me limp
and stretched out upon the pillows
Breathless
As the aftershocks of coming ran through me
and your name was upon my lips

There are currents that sustain me
Those in meditation that rock me open
and drop me into stillness
before I am tossed upon the shore of conscious
thought
When they have had their way with me

The currents of individual Deities that I work with
and for
Each an aspect a Person with particular aspects and gifts
a particular flavor for want of a better expression
Each has a taste that all of what I am responds to
and welcomes into shared space within
upon occasion
Their downloads into my being
Bring new transformation and understanding

This current between you and me though
is like the sacred waters of a crashing rapids
Picking me up and carrying me
or tossing me restlessly upon its furious rush
as my body surrenders and itself liquefies
before being dropped on the other side
Into a deep still pool where the rest is sweet
and our union has caressed every part of me

More often though the current is fiery
Electrical
Hot and stimulating
Expansive
It fills the physical body only to go on
and caress and tweak the astral
the third eye opens and dances with the swirling centers
above and below it
Your energy tantalizes it pokes it opens
it teases it brings out my inner fire
and my outer as ignition explodes
and I ride our current in bliss

About Concrescent Letters

Concrescent Letters is dedicated to publishing unique works of Poetry and Prose. It takes advantage of the recent revolution in publishing technology and economics to bring forth works that, previously, might only have been circulated privately.

Now, we are growing the future together.

Colophon

This book is made of Mistral and Dakota, using Adobe InDesign. The cover was designed, the body was set by Sam Webster.

Visit our website at
www.Concrescent.net

www.ingramcontent.com/pod-product-compliance
Lightning Source LLC
Chambersburg PA
CBHW030504100426
42813CB00002B/330